AF348456

THE TERRIBLE STORMS OF 2005

THE TERRIBLE STORMS OF 2005

Hurricane Katrina & Hurricane Rita

Edited by TRENT ANGERS

Acadian House
PUBLISHING
Lafayette, Louisiana

The Acadian House Publishing Speakers Bureau can bring authors to your live event. For more information or to book an author, contact Acadian House Publishing at (337) 235-8851, Ext. 104, or info@acadianhouse.com.

Library of Congress Cataloging-in-Publication Data

The terrible storms of 2005 : Hurricane Katrina & Hurricane Rita / edited by Trent Angers.
    pages cm
Includes bibliographical references and index.
ISBN-13: 978-0-925417-94-7
ISBN-10: 0-925417-94-7 (hardcover : alk. paper) 1. Hurricane Katrina, 2005.
2. Hurricane Rita, 2005. 3. Disasters--Louisiana--History--21st century.
4. New Orleans (La.)--History--21st century. I. Angers, Trent, editor.
HV636 2005 .L8 T435 2015
363.34'92209763--dc23
    2015029954

♦ Published by Acadian House Publishing, Lafayette, Louisiana
  (Edited by Trent Angers; editorial assistance and research by
  Darlene Smith; interior pre-press production by Charlotte Huggins)
♦ Cover design and production by Glenn Noya, New Orleans, Louisiana
♦ Map work by Don Fields, Lafayette, Louisiana, and Angelina Leger,
  Lafayette, Louisiana
♦ Printed by Sheridan Books, Chelsea, Michigan

Double trouble

August 29, 2005, was the worst day in the lives of many in southeast Louisiana and southwest Mississippi. It's the day when Hurricane Katrina blew ashore, leading to the deaths of more than 1,800 people, mostly in the greater New Orleans area.

About a month later, on September 24, the people of southwest Louisiana and southeast Texas experienced a disaster of their own when Hurricane Rita slammed into this coastal area with a vengeance. The powerful storm flattened the town of Cameron, drowned thousands of cattle, and took the lives of about 100 people who were caught up in the evacuation of the Galveston/Houston area.

We at *Acadiana Profile* Magazine, based in Lafayette, La., were just out of the reach of either storm. I was editor and publisher of the magazine at the time, a position I held for 36 years in all, through 2010.

My staff and I watched closely as TV reporters announced that Katrina had veered off to the east of New Orleans and that the city had been spared the worst. But then came news that the levees designed to protect the city were failing, and that the oversized bowl that is New Orleans was filling up with water.

A few weeks later, while we were writing and editing stories for an *Acadiana Profile* Special Report on Katrina, we got word that another dangerous hurricane, a Category 5, was in the Gulf and headed for southeast Texas or possibly southwest Louisiana.

If it were to hit our state, the magazine's focus on the Katrina story would have to be divided, split between two hurricanes, thus compounding the task of reporting and editing.

It was an exciting time to be a journalist in our part of the country, and at the same time mind-boggling, considering the enormity of the tragedies at hand.

When Rita did hit southwest Louisiana, we, like others in the media, were deluged with information about the dual disasters.

It was hard to take it all in – and even harder to sort it out. I had never seen anything like this double whammy.

To achieve the best coverage possible, we conducted numerous interviews, hired freelancers, rode herd on the Associated Press news wire, and sifted through a flood of news releases from various sources. We gathered and evaluated countless photographs from rescuers, from the Associated Press and from several government agencies.

In the end, we published not one but five Special Reports in *Acadiana Profile*. We ran dozens of article, scores of photographs and several maps and other graphics in an effort to present as many aspects of this story as we could. And that's what appears in the pages of this book: a lightly re-edited version of the material originally published in the 2005-07 magazine series titled "The Terrible Storms of 2005."

– Trent Angers

On the front lines
of Katrina and Rita

By Lt. General Russel L. Honoré
(U.S. Army, Retired)

Hurricane Katrina is frequently described as "one of the worst natural disasters in U.S. history," with more than 1,800 lives lost as a result of this killer storm and the flooding that resulted. Hurricane Rita, an even more powerful storm when it came ashore a month later on the opposite side of south Louisiana, annihilated the coastal town of Cameron, destroying virtually every building in the community except the courthouse.

In Cameron, everything was gone – broken to bits, floated out into the marshes or sucked out to sea. It looked like a war zone.

On the following pages is an accurate depiction of the tragic events that befell the people of the Gulf Coast in the sweltering heat of August and September of 2005.

But as bad as it was for Cameron and New Orleans, it could have been a lot worse. In a way, we got lucky, believe it or not! Katrina was headed straight for New Orleans then veered off to the east. Had New Orleans taken a direct hit, the property damage and death toll due to high winds could have added greatly to the damage done by the flooding.

Rita had Galveston/Houston in its crosshairs then curved to the east, toward the thinly populated southwest corner of Louisiana. Had Rita scored a direct hit on the densely populated Texas cities, that damage could have been massive, particularly in the flood-prone metropolis of Houston.

I witnessed Katrina and Rita's destruction firsthand, up close and personal, because it was my job to track these hurricanes then to bring in the troops to provide search-and-rescue, food and water, and evacuation assistance to storm victims. As Commander of Joint Task Force Katrina, I had under my command 20,000 troops (Army, Air Force, Navy and Marines), 200 helicopters, 20 ships and numerous vehicles.

Our mission for Katrina was to provide military assistance to civilian authorities. We worked in collaboration with the National Guard, who were under the command of Louisiana Governor Kathleen Blanco.

Our mission for Hurricane Rita was essentially the same, but the tasks at hand proved to be vastly different due to the difference in density of populations, the kinds of damage inflicted by the two storms, and the numbers of people who did and didn't evacuate in advance of the storms.

The population of the greater New Orleans area (including St. Bernard and Plaquemines parishes) was about 500,000 at the time; plus, there were about 100,000 more on the western Mississippi Gulf Coast. A majority of the Mississippi people in Katrina's path evacuated on their own, as ordered. But it was a different story for the people living in New Orleans; at least 70,000 had to be evacuated after the storm.

On the other hand, when we went into Cameron right after Rita came through, we found only one man who had stayed behind. One man. He was in the courthouse, which weathered the storm relatively well. Additionally, we air-lifted about 100 people who were stranded on Pecan Island because they hadn't gotten out before the roads flooded.

So, obviously, the density of the population and the topography of the land were huge factors in the disparity in the death tolls from those two storms. With Rita, the storm surge came in, did its damage, then receded. With Katrina, the water flooded New Orleans but couldn't drain off because the city is way below sea level, so the water remained and had to be pumped out – which was a major operation, to say the least.

After all was said and done in New Orleans, at least 50,000 people were rescued by civilian and military personnel, using boats, airboats, Army trucks, helicopters, etc. Some were trapped in their homes, some in their attics, on rooftops, even in trees. Many were wading through water up to their knees, or to their waists, even up to their chins.

Besides the people we rescued, thousands of lives were saved by neighbors, friends and family members, as well as volunteers who came to the city from out of town. They brought boats and airboats and a steadfast determination to help their neighbors in need – just as Americans have always done. It was inspiring to see these good-hearted people, this humanitarian army, coming in day after day. Their compensation was simply the knowledge that they had helped their fellow citizens in their hour of need.

The stories of many of these heroic people can be found in this book. One of my favorites is titled "The Cajun Navy," which is about the group who came to the flooded city with their boats from Lafayette, Abbeville, Lake Charles and other south Louisiana communities. Another chapter that impresses me is titled "An Airboat on the Streets of New Orleans," which tells of a Breaux Bridge couple who brought in their airboat and rescued hundreds of desperate people.

We've all heard – and many of us have seen – that disasters like these bring out the best in some people and the worst in others. That's a fact, and we saw both kinds of behavior in the wakes of these terrible storms.

What we saw in New Orleans – from the front lines – was devastation of biblical proportions.

What we saw in the people who came to help was America at its finest.

Louisiana Gulf Coast slammed by two major hurricanes in less than a month

Ushering in the worst natural disaster in U.S. history, Hurricane Katrina came ashore over the wetlands of southeast Louisiana on the morning of August 29, 2005, then veered to the east and mowed down hundreds of homes and businesses on the Mississippi Gulf Coast. The storm's massive tidal surge raised the water in Lake Pontchartrain, causing the failure of the levee system that protects New Orleans. The city flooded and panic ensued as thousands were trapped in their homes by the rising water.

Less than a month later, on the morning of September 24, a second major storm named Hurricane Rita mauled and flooded the southwest corner of Louisiana, annihilating the towns of Cameron and Grand Chenier and causing extensive damage in Lake Charles and Sulphur. The storm also ravaged southeast Texas, shutting down oil refineries and disrupting people's lives in a profound way.

The tidal surges from these two storms caused floods in every parish in coastal Louisiana, destroying homes and camps; drowning people, pets and livestock; ruining sugarcane and other crops; and damaging or sinking sailboats, yachts, shrimp trawlers and workboats of every description.

The hurricanes brought down trees and power lines;

wiped many homes and businesses off the face of the earth, literally; shut down schools for days or weeks or longer; disrupted businesses totally and in many cases permanently; and sent tens of thousands of people to the food stamp and unemployment lines. Many were left homeless, jobless, hopeless and penniless.

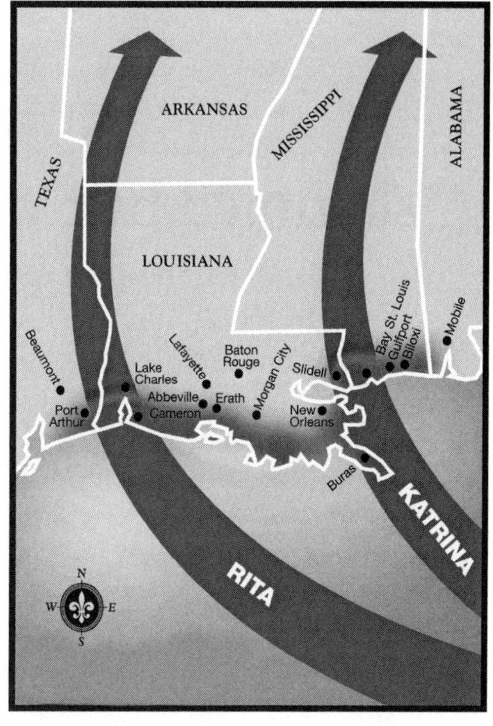

For many, the emotional trauma was compounded by the death of family members, friends, and/or pets. Hundreds of families were separated during the post-hurricane evacuation from New Orleans.

The storm displaced people of every age, every race, every occupation: school children and their teachers; college professors and students; business people; football players; Jackson Square artists; jazz musicians; famous chefs; strippers, bartenders and bouncers; priests and religious sisters and brothers; cops, robbers and prisoners; newlyweds and the newly separated; already-homeless men and women and children; the rich and well-heeled, as well as the poor and downtrodden.

Hurricane Katrina flushed all of them out of New Orleans, some for awhile, some forever. Some left on buses or trains; a small number went by plane; but the masses left by car in the bumper-to-bumper traffic that was a nightmare in its own right.

Images of destruction

Television news programs broadcast memorable images of the destruction and aftermath of these massive storms: splintered houses, missing houses in Biloxi; sailboats stacked up in a pile, like so many sardines; people in New Orleans wading through chest-high floodwater, heading for higher ground, children on their shoulders, pets in their arms, all the people carrying plastic bags containing their belongings.

There were unforgettable pictures of people standing on rooftops, baking in the sun, desperate to be rescued, waving white towels or T-shirts, scrambling for life, trying to get a ride. And there were throngs of people, people who couldn't or wouldn't get out of town before the hurricane, waiting for a bus to come for them at the Superdome or at the Convention Center.

The news shows presented haunting images of drowned cattle floating in the floodwaters somewhere south of Lake Charles and somewhere south of Abbeville, as well as pictures of flooded and crippled oil refineries in the Lake Charles-Beaumont area.

Hurricane Katrina's floodwaters covered 75 to 80 percent of New Orleans, with water reaching to the ceilings of houses in many neighborhoods, and even higher in others. It was a flood of biblical proportions; for many, it was indeed the end of the world as they knew it.

As the water rose, thousands of New Orleans area people made their way into their attics, only to find that the water was continuing to rise. Even in some attics, the water was knee-deep, then waist-deep, then chest-deep, then chin-deep. Some kicked their way out through the air vents at the peak of the roof; others didn't have the strength to do so. Some had the presence of mind to bring axes, hammers or crowbars with them into the attic, and they knocked holes in their roofs and escaped through them.

Heroic rescues by boat, airboat and helicopter

Many thousands avoided the attics altogether and climbed onto their roofs from outside of their houses. They were subsequently rescued by the U.S. Coast Guard or others. Using helicopters, the Coast Guard lowered men on wire lines to the rooftops; they would secure the people in a basket or on a seat and signal those in the helicopter to hoist them up. Thousands were rescued in this fashion.

Thousands of others were rescued by boat or by airboat. Participating in these heroic efforts were the Coast Guard, National Guard, New Orleans police, various sheriff's departments and civilians.

Acadian Ambulance Service and Air Med, with the help of ambulance companies from several states, evacuated patients from seven New Orleans hospitals, including Tulane Medical Center, Charity Hospital, Touro Infirmary and Children's Hospital. The airlifts had to be stopped temporarily because of reports of sniper fire in the immediate area.

As rescue efforts continued, thousands of citizens were crowding into the Convention Center in downtown New Orleans. Some were dropped off by helicopter after being rescued from their flooded homes; others waded out of their neighborhoods and walked the rest of the way to the facility. Thousands of people made their way to the already-crowded Superdome, while others were brought - by boat or helicopter - to Causeway Boulevard or to the raised spans of Interstate 10 and Interstate 610.

The breakdown of law and order

Unfortunately, food and water were slow in coming to these stranded and desperate people - on the interstates, in the Superdome and at the Convention Center. Federal, State and local governments - which seemed unprepared, out of focus and not in sync with one another – all bore responsibility for this ineffectual response to the needs of these increasingly desperate, increasingly angry people.

The poor response on the part of government at all levels – a response that President Bush referred to as "unacceptable" – contributed to the breakdown of law and order in New Orleans. For a while, the city was in a state of anarchy, with rampant looting, reports of arson, murders, rapes and unbounded civil unrest and chaos. Then came the sniping.

Rescue workers who were evacuating residents from their houses and helicopter pilots airlifting critically ill patients from downtown hospitals heard sniper fire while on their missions.

When the sniping started and the looting became widespread and totally out of hand, New Orleans police had to be pulled off of search-and-rescue operations and reassigned to simple law enforcement duties in an effort to restore law and order in the city. But the problems were too much for the local police, who were already overextended, exhausted and distracted by reports of fellow officers deserting the force in an hour of extreme need.

Subsequently, additional National Guard troops were brought in – under the command of Lt. Gen. Russel Honoré (a Louisiana native) – and the anarchy subsided as the soldiers fanned out across the city. The Guard helped to restore law and order and assisted in the rescue effort.

Human kindness overflowing

This disaster, like many others, was a time of death, destruction, depression, confusion and high anxiety. While it brought out the absolute worst in some people, it clearly brought out the very best in many more. It revealed the depths to which some people will sink to serve their own interests or to violently express their anger and frustration, and the heights to which others will rise to serve their fellowman.

Aside from the massive and much-publicized humanitarian

relief effort spearheaded by the American Red Cross and FEMA, countless acts of kindness and compassion toward evacuees continue to be observed in these trying times. For instance:

• A five-car caravan with 12 people, four dogs, two cats and two turtles stopped at a Breaux Bridge gas station off I-10. Headed by a 74-year-old widow named Bobbie Spiers, they were attempting to sleep in their vehicles after a grueling 10-hour drive away from the path of the coming hurricane.

A man from Parks, in St. Martin Parish, walked up to one of the cars and asked the driver, "Do y'all need a place to stay?" The driver answered in the affirmative, and the local man said, "Follow me." So he led the caravan to his house, where they were able to relax, sleep and eat.

Mrs. Spiers and her group were amazed at the kindness and trusting nature of their host, Chad Lavergne.

"Oh, my God, I didn't know people like that existed anywhere in the world," Mrs. Spiers remarked.

• Fifty evacuees from the New Orleans area were crowded into 14 of the 19 rooms at Beno's Motel in St. Martinville. The news traveled quickly around the community, and soon the evacuees were enjoying free meals from Joyce's Supermarket Cafeteria, Durand Grocery and the St. Martin Parish Sheriff's Office.

The room rate, ordinarily modest, was reduced further for these special guests. Owner Reuben "Beno" Talley marked on each of the 14 bills "N/C" – no charge.

• A shelter on the campus of Nicholls State University in Thibodaux wouldn't allow pets in, so those with animals were hanging around outside the building with their furry friends.

The priest with the St. Thomas Aquinas Catholic Center on campus, Rev. Jim Morrison, observed the dejected-looking people with their pets and invited them – all 130 people and all their pets – to the Catholic Center.

The invitees included all sorts of dogs and cats, plus birds and a pot-bellied pig. Fr. Morrison, a dog owner himself, proclaimed at the sight (which looked very much like Noah's ark):

"Our altar has never been adorned more beautifully than it is with these people and their animals seeking the sanctuary of God."

–*Trent Angers,*
Editor

Contents

(Continued)

THE TERRIBLE STORMS OF 2005

PART 1
HURRICANE KATRINA

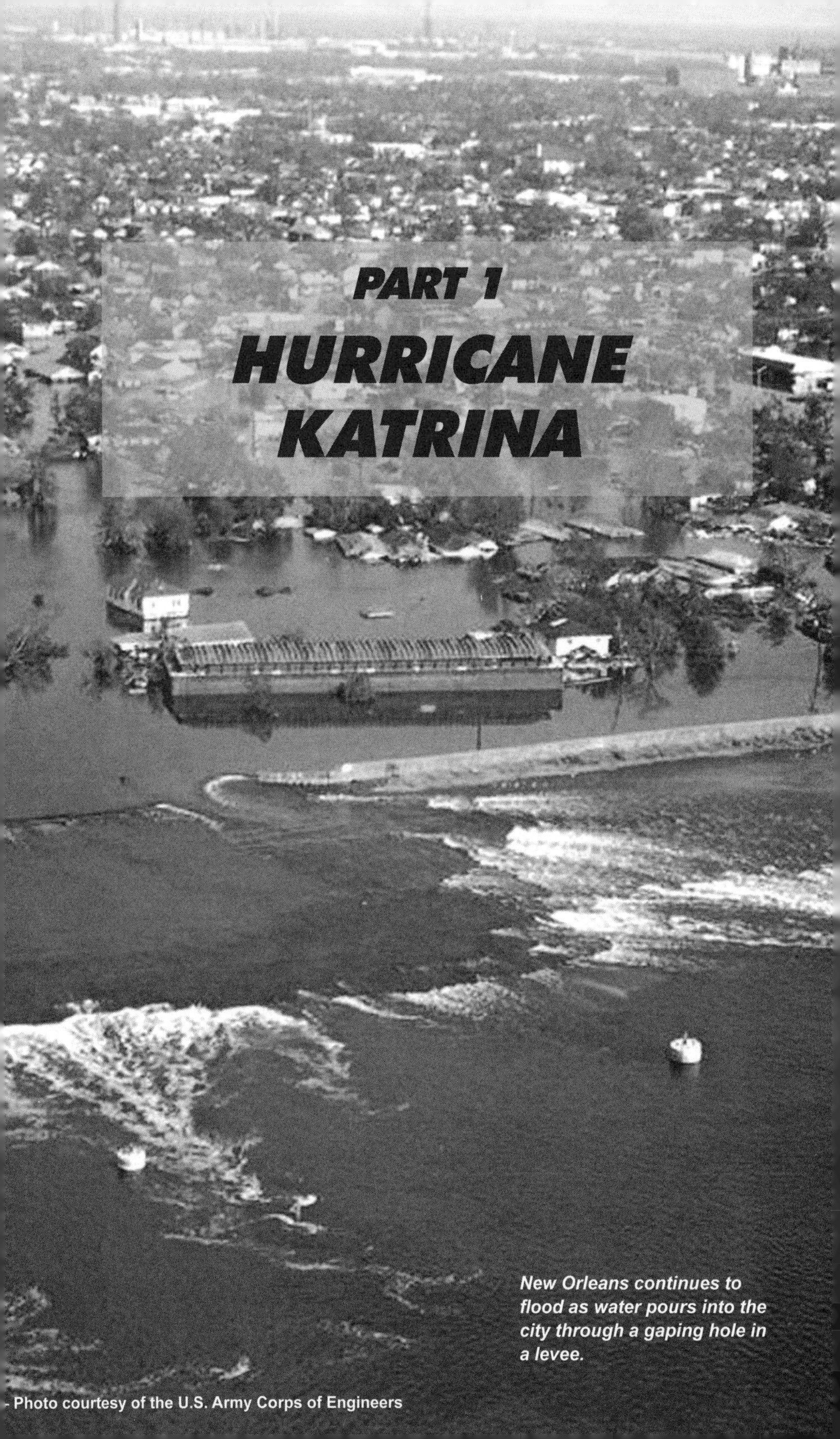

New Orleans continues to flood as water pours into the city through a gaping hole in a levee.

Photo courtesy of the U.S. Army Corps of Engineers

New Orleans' descent into anarchy

Amid violence, squalor and feelings of abandonment,
hurricane victims were desperate to get out of
'The City That Care Forgot.'

New Orleans descended into anarchy on Thursday Sept. 1, 2005, as corpses lay abandoned in street medians, fights and fires broke out, and storm survivors battled for seats on the buses that would carry them away from the chaos. The tired and hungry seethed, saying they had been forsaken.

"I'm not sure I'm going to get out of here alive," said Canadian tourist Larry Mitzel, who handed a reporter his business card in case he goes missing. "I'm scared of riots. I'm scared of the locals. We might get caught in the crossfire."

Four days after Hurricane Katrina roared in with a devastating blow, the frustration, fear and anger mounted, despite the promise of 1,400 National Guardsmen a day to stop the looting, plans for a $10 billion recovery bill in Congress, and a government relief effort President Bush called the biggest in U.S. history.

New Orleans' top emergency management official called that effort a "national disgrace" and questioned when reinforcements would actually reach the increasingly lawless city.

About 15,000 to 20,000 people who had taken shelter at New Orleans Convention Center grew increasingly hostile after waiting for buses for days amid the filth and the dead. Police Chief Eddie Compass said there was such a crush around a squad of 88 officers that they retreated when they went in to check out reports of assaults.

"We have individuals who are getting raped, we have individuals who are getting beaten," Compass said. "Tourists are walking in that direction and they are getting preyed upon."

A military helicopter tried to land at the Convention Center several times to drop off food and water. But the rushing crowd forced the chopper to back off. Troopers then tossed the supplies to the crowd from 10 feet off the ground and flew away.

In hopes of defusing the situation at the Convention Center, Mayor Ray Nagin gave the refugees permission to march across the bridge to the city's unflooded west bank for whatever relief they could find. But the bedlam made that difficult.

"This is a desperate SOS," Nagin said in a statement. "Right now we are out of resources at the Convention Center and don't anticipate enough buses."

At least seven bodies were scattered outside the Convention Center, a makeshift staging area for those rescued from rooftops, attics and highways. The sidewalks were packed with people without food, water or medical care, and with no sign of law enforcement.

An old man in a chaise lounge lay dead in a grassy median as hungry babies wailed around him. Around the corner, an elderly woman lay dead in her wheelchair, covered up by a blanket, and another body lay beside her wrapped in a sheet.

"I don't treat my dog like that," 47-year-old Daniel Edwards said as he pointed at the woman in the wheelchair.

"You can do everything for other countries, but you can't do nothing for your own people," he added. "You can go overseas with the military, but you can't get them down here."

The street outside the center, above the floodwaters, smelled of urine and feces, and was choked with dirty diapers, old bottles and garbage.

"They've been teasing us with buses for four days," Edwards said. "They're telling us they're going to come get us one day, and then they don't show up."

Every so often, an armored State Police vehicle cruised in front of the Convention Center with four or five officers in riot gear with automatic weapons. But there was no sign of help from the National Guard.

At one point the crowd began to chant, "We want help! We want help!" Later, a woman, screaming, went on the front steps of the Convention Center and led the crowd in reciting the 23rd Psalm, "The Lord is my shepherd...."

"We are out here like pure animals," Issac Clark said. "We've got people dying out here. Two babies have died, a woman died, a man died," said Helen Cheek. "We haven't had no food, we haven't had no water, we haven't had nothing. They just brought us here and dropped us."

Tourist Debbie Durso of Washington, Mich., said she asked a police officer for assistance and his response was, "Go to hell! It's every man for himself!"

"This is just insanity," she said. "We have no food, no water... all these trucks and buses go by and they do nothing but wave."

FEMA director Michael Brown said his agency just learned about the situation at the Convention Center Thursday Sept. 1 and quickly scrambled to provide food, water and medical care and remove the corpses.

At the hot and stinking Superdome, where 30,000 were being evacuated by bus to the Houston Astrodome, fistfights and fires erupted amid a seething sea of tense, suffering people who waited in lines that stretched half a mile to board yellow school buses.

After a traffic jam kept buses from arriving for nearly four hours, a near-riot broke out in the scramble to get on the buses that finally did show up, with a group of refugees breaking through a line of heavily armed National Guardsmen.

One military policeman was shot in the leg as he and a man scuffled for the MP's rifle, police Capt. Ernie Demmo said. The man was arrested.

Some of those among the mostly poor crowd had been in the dome for four days without air conditioning, working toilets or a place to bathe. An ambulance service airlifting the sick and injured out of the Superdome suspended flights as too dangerous after it was reported that a bullet was fired at a military helicopter.

"If they're just taking us anywhere, just anywhere, I say, 'Praise God,'" said refugee John Phillip. "Nothing could be worse than what we've been through."

By Thursday evening, 11 hours after the military began evacuating the Superdome, the arena held 10,000 more people than it did at dawn. National Guard Capt. John Pollard said evacuees from around the city poured into the Superdome and swelled the crowd to about 30,000 because they believed the dome was the best place to get a ride out of town.

As he watched a line snaking for blocks through ankle-deep waters, New Orleans' emergency operations chief Terry Ebbert blamed the inadequate response on the Federal Emergency Management Agency (FEMA).

"This is not a FEMA operation; I haven't seen a single FEMA guy," he said. "We can send massive amounts of aid to tsunami victims, but we can't bail out the city of New Orleans."

FEMA officials said some operations had to be suspended in areas where gunfire had broken out, but were working overtime to feed people and restore order.

– The Associated Press

'It's time for action, not press conferences'

New Orleans Mayor Ray Nagin pleads for State and Federal help in WWL radio interview as citizens are drowning in the flood.

Three days after Hurricane Katrina had swamped south Louisiana, leaving death, destruction and chaos in her wake, New Orleans Mayor Ray Nagin criticized the Federal and State governments for their slow pace in relief efforts. In an exclusive interview with WWL correspondent Garland Robinette on September 1, the 49-year-old mayor unloaded on officials in an expletive-filled rant that caught the attention of national commentators throughout the country.

The interview, conducted some hours after Nagin's conversation with President Bush – who had just viewed the damage from Air Force One – captured the frustration and anger present in the beleaguered city.

Following are excerpts from that interview.

* * * * *

"I told (the President) we had an incredible crisis here and that his flying over in Air Force One does not do it justice. And that I have been all around this city, and I am very frustrated because we are not able to marshal resources – and we're out-manned in just about every respect.

"You know the reason why the looters got out of control? Because we had most of our resources saving people, thousands of people that were stuck in attics, man, old ladies.... You pull off the doggone ventilator vent and you look down there and they're standing in there in water up to their freaking necks.

"And they don't have a clue what's going on down here. They flew down here one time two days after the doggone event was over with TV cameras, AP reporters...."

Glad to see Lt. Gen. Honoré

"Now, I will tell you this – and I give the President some credit on this – he sent one John Wayne dude down here that can get some stuff done, and his name is [Lt.] Gen. [Russel] Honoré. And he came off the doggone chopper, and he started cussing and people started moving. And he's getting some stuff done. They ought to give that guy – if they don't want to give it to me – give him full authority to get the job done, and we can save some people."

On the need for troops and buses

"I need reinforcements, I need troops, man. I need 500 buses.... One of the briefings we had, they were talking about getting public school bus drivers to come down here and bus people out.

"I'm like, 'You got to be kidding me! This is a national disaster. Get every doggone Greyhound bus line in the country and get their asses moving to New Orleans.' They're thinking small, man. And this is a major, major, major deal. And I can't emphasize it enough.

"This is crazy! I've got 15,000 to 20,000 people over at the convention center. It's bursting at the seams....

"It's awful down here, man."

A cry for help

"We said, please, please take care of this. We don't care what you do. Figure it out. Everybody – the governor, Homeland Security, FEMA – you name it, we said it. And they allowed that pumping station next to Pumping Station 6 to go under water. Our sewage and water board people ... stayed there and endangered their lives. And what happened when that pumping station went down, the water started flowing again in the city, and it starting getting to levels that probably killed more people....

"You know, in a state of emergency, man, you are creative, you figure out ways to get stuff done. Then they told me that they went overnight, and they built 17 concrete structures and they had the pulleys on them and they were going to drop them. I flew over that thing yesterday, and it's in the same shape that it was after the storm hit. There is nothing happening! And they're feeding the public a line of bull and they're spinning, and people are dying down here."

On anarchy and the need for martial law

"We called for martial law when we realized that the looting was getting out of control. And we redirected all of our police officers back to patrolling the streets. They were dead-tired from saving people, but they worked all night because we thought this thing was going to blow wide open last night. And so we redirected all of our resources.... I'm not sure if we can do that another night with the current resources. They're showing all these reports of people looting and doing all that weird stuff... but people are desperate and they're trying to find food and water, the majority of them.

"Now you got some knuckleheads out there, and they are taking advantage of this lawless... situation where, you know, we can't really control it. And they're doing some awful, awful things. But that's a small majority of the people. Most people are looking to try and survive.

"And nobody's talked about this, (but) drugs flowed in and out of New Orleans and the surrounding metropolitan area so freely it was scary to me – and that's why we were having the escalation in murders. People don't want to talk about this, but I'm going to talk about it. You have drug addicts that are now walking around this city looking for a fix, and that's the reason why they were breaking in hospitals and drugstores. They're looking for something to take the edge off.... And right now, they don't have anything to take the edge off. And they've probably found guns. So what you're seeing is drug-starving, crazy addicts, drug addicts, that are wreaking havoc. And we don't have the manpower to adequately deal with it. We can only target certain sections of the city and form a perimeter around them and hope to God that we're not overrun."

Isn't New Orleans worth an immediate response from the government?

"Well, did the tsunami victims request? Did it go through a formal process to request? Did the Iraqi people request that we go in there? Did they ask us to go in there? What is more important?

"But we authorized $8 billion to go to Iraq lickety-quick. After 9/11, we gave the President unprecedented powers lickety-quick to take care of New York and other places. Now, you mean to tell me that a place where most of your oil is coming through... a place that is so unique that when you mention New Orleans anywhere around the world, everybody's eyes light up, ... you mean to tell me that a place where you probably have thousands of people that have died and thousands more that are dying every day, that we can't figure out a way to authorize the resources that we need? Come on, man....

"And I don't know whose problem it is. I don't know whether it's the governor's problem. I don't know whether it's the President's problem, but somebody needs to get their ass on a plane and sit down, the two of them, and figure this out right now."

It's time for action, not press conferences

"Organize people to write letters and make calls to their

congressmen, to the President, to the governor. Flood their dog-gone offices with requests to do something. This is ridiculous.

"I don't want to see anybody do anymore ... press confer-ences. Put a moratorium on press conferences. Don't do an-other press conference until the resources are in this city. And then come down to this city and stand with us when there are military trucks and troops that we can't even count.

"Don't tell me 40,000 people are coming here. They're *not* here. It's too doggone late. Now get off your asses and do something, and let's fix the biggest ... crisis in the history of this country."

– Transcription provided by Don Allen

The Cajun Navy

Soon after Hurricane Katrina struck the Gulf Coast, thousands of Louisianians and people from other parts of the U.S. headed for New Orleans to rescue victims of the flood. Among these first responders were two loosely organized groups – one from the Lafayette area and one from the Lake Charles area – who hitched up their boats and traveled in caravans to the flood zone. They became known as 'The Cajun Navy.' They will go down in history as heroes, one and all.

By Jefferson Hennessy

Two days after Hurricane Katrina came ashore and caused breaks in New Orleans' levee system, State Sen. Nick Gautreaux of Abbeville drove to a restaurant in Broussard to meet a friend for lunch. While waiting for his friend to arrive, the senator became transfixed by the disturbing images of devastation he was watching on television.

He saw pictures of flooding on an unprecedented scale in New Orleans and adjacent St. Bernard Parish, where countless neighborhoods were submerged under as much as 20 feet of water from Lake Pontchartrain and from the storm surge.

Television reports were saying that on the previous day, three New Orleans canal levees were breached in the early morning hours while Hurricane Katrina was roaring through the city, knocking over oak trees, breaking power lines, smashing homes, and tossing seagoing vessels ashore like they were toy boats.

Residents of St. Bernard Parish who did not evacuate had been overwhelmed by 20 feet of water in less than 20 minutes. The storm surge knocked out electrical power and pushed raw sewage into the rising tide.

St. Bernard Parish, an area of 680 square miles with a population of 67,000, suffered a one-two punch – raging floodwater from breached levees in New Orleans and a massive storm surge that entered unobstructed through the Mississippi River Gulf Outlet – completely swamping homes and businesses too quickly for many who were unable to react and escape alive. Most of the dead were elderly or disabled.

The next morning, live television images showed the sun shining brightly on tranquil floodwaters through a calm, clear sky, revealing a thoroughly inundated New Orleans and St. Bernard Parish. Thousands of local residents who stayed behind, either by choice or because of their inability to leave, were now trapped on their rooftops and were desperate to escape, or had taken shelter in their attics, which proved to be dark, deadly traps for many who were drowned as the murky surge waters rose.

While watching the shocking images of devastation and desperate people on television at the restaurant in Broussard, Sen. Gautreaux resolved to do something to help.

"I have to do something to help those people. We can't just stand around and watch those people on their rooftops," he said to his friend Randy Breaux, a Lafayette insurance agent.

He explained he wanted to organize a citizen flotilla of hundreds of boats with hundreds of volunteers and drive to New Orleans to rescue people trapped on their roofs.

"I told Randy what I wanted to do, and he asked me, 'Are you crazy?' I said to him, 'We're going to get it together; watch what happens. Randy ended up coming with me," Gautreaux says.

While driving to his office in Abbeville, with his plan clearly in mind, Gautreaux telephoned his office and directed his assistants to alert the local news media and tell them what he intended to do.

Then, Gautreaux sent a text message on his Blackberry to State Sen. Walter Boasso, a lifelong resident of St. Bernard

Parish, to get the latest news about how things were going in that parish, and to ask what he could do to help. Attempts to telephone Boasso by cell phone were unsuccessful.

Boasso, who had been rescuing people from rooftops in St. Bernard since the previous afternoon, replied with a short, chilling text message:

"My people are dying. Please send help."

"Don't worry. Help is on the way," Gautreaux replied.

That afternoon two Lafayette-based TV stations, KATC and KLFY, carried Gautreaux's urgent appeal to the public: *Every able-bodied citizen with a boat is invited to show up at the Acadiana Mall on Johnston Street in Lafayette by 5 o'clock tomorrow morning and drive to New Orleans to help rescue stranded flood victims.*

He gave out the number to his office, and within an hour 200 phone calls came in. The rescue mission was on.

When Gautreaux arrived at the Acadiana Mall in the early hours of Wednesday morning he was stunned by what he saw. The parking lot was filled with boats and trucks of all shapes and sizes and hundreds of people willing to help rescue their fellow Louisiana citizens.

"The great thing about it was it was typical Louisiana," Gautreaux said later. "We had doctors, lawyers, college students, nurses, working class people, and offshore oilfield workers who had the day off because of the hurricane. We even had a person who bought a brand new boat and motor that day so he could go with us. I thought that was great. It's part of our Cajun heritage to help our neighbor. When New Orleans needed help we were there to help them."

Participants in Gautreaux's citizen flotilla came from all over south Louisiana: Ville Platte, Lake Charles, Abbeville, Erath, New Iberia, Maurice, Carencro, Jennings, Opelousas and other communities. Eyewitness estimates put the number of boats between 300 and 500, and the number of volunteers at 600 to 800.

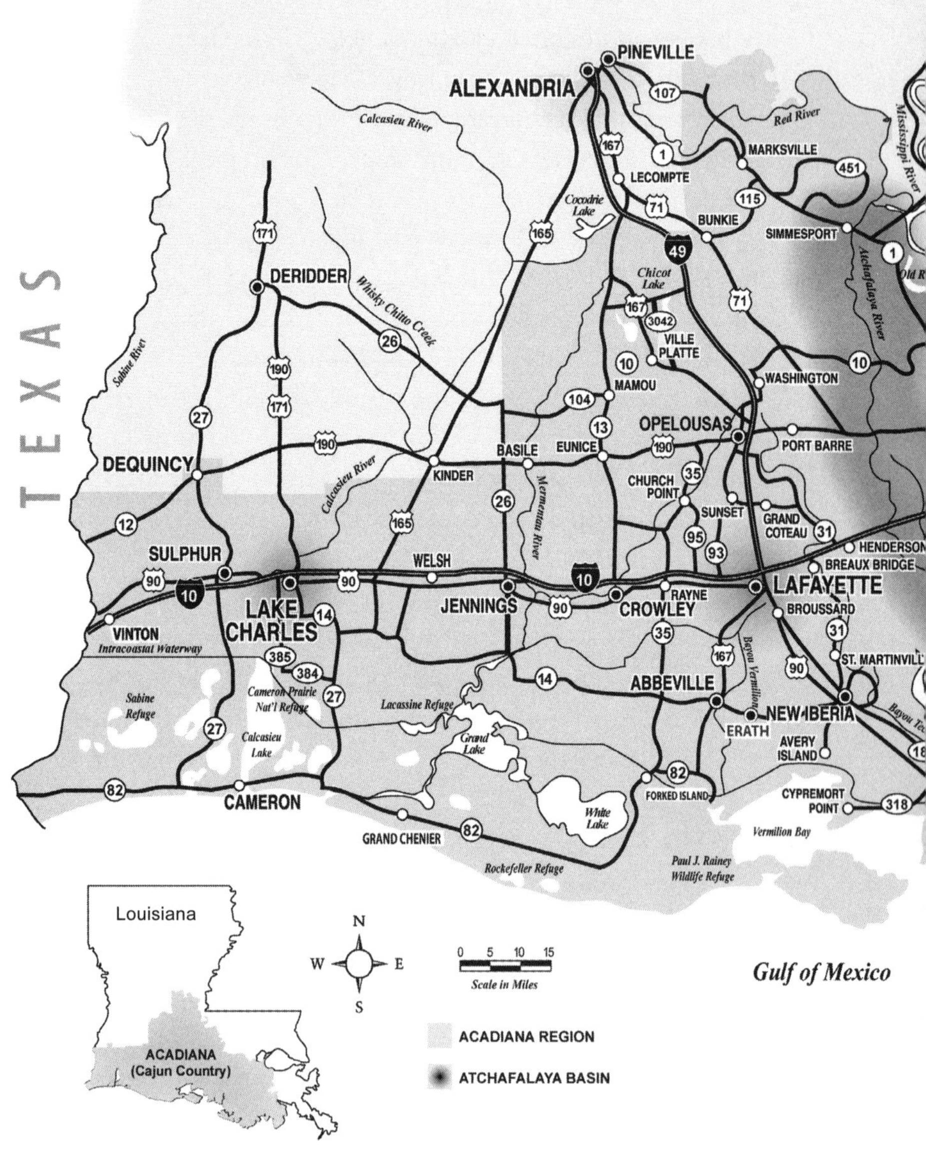

TEXAS
PINEVILLE
ALEXANDRIA
Calcasieu River
Red River
107
167
1
MARKSVILLE
451
LECOMPTE
Cocodrie Lake
71
BUNKIE
115
SIMMESPORT
Mississippi River
165
171
49
Atchafalaya River
1
Old R.
DERIDDER
Whisky Chitto Creek
Chicot Lake
167
26
3042
VILLE PLATTE
71
10
190
MAMOU
10
WASHINGTON
Sabine River
104
171
27
190
13
OPELOUSAS
PORT BARRE
DEQUINCY
190
BASILE
EUNICE
190
35
KINDER
CHURCH POINT
Calcasieu River
SUNSET
GRAND COTEAU
31
HENDERSON
12
Mermentau River
26
95
93
BREAUX BRIDGE
SULPHUR
165
WELSH
10
LAFAYETTE
90
90
90
BROUSSARD
10
RAYNE
VINTON
Intracoastal Waterway
14
JENNINGS
90
CROWLEY
31
LAKE CHARLES
35
ST. MARTINVILLE
385
167
90
384
14
ABBEVILLE
Bayou Vermilion
Sabine Refuge
27
Cameron Prairie Nat'l Refuge
Lacassine Refuge
NEW IBERIA
18
27
Calcasieu Lake
Grand Lake
ERATH
AVERY ISLAND
Bayou Teche
82
FORKED ISLAND
82
CYPREMORT POINT
318
CAMERON
White Lake
Vermilion Bay
GRAND CHENIER
82
Rockefeller Refuge
Paul J. Rainey Wildlife Refuge
Louisiana
N
W E
S
0 5 10 15
Scale in Miles
Gulf of Mexico
ACADIANA (Cajun Country)
ACADIANA REGION
ATCHAFALAYA BASIN

South Louisiana

This is a region of the United States that has seen more than its share of hurricanes since the start of the 20th century. Included are the two terrible storms of 2005: **Katrina**, that left more than 1,800 people dead in and around New Orleans and southwest Mississippi; and **Rita**, which demolished Cameron, completely destroying or heavily damaging every structure in town except for the courthouse and the water tower.

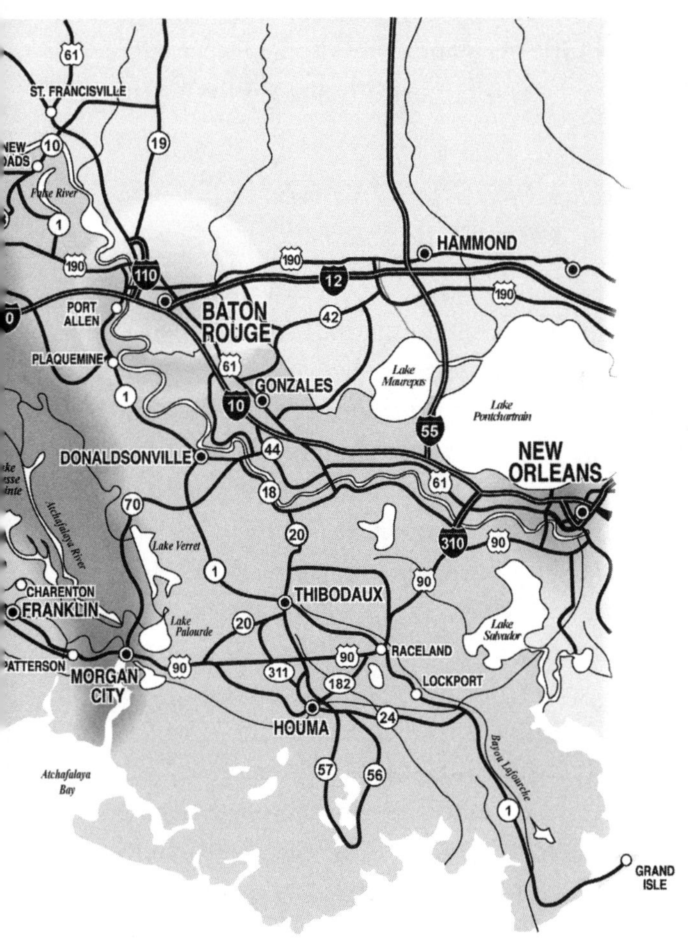

Although Gautreaux was quite pleased with the turnout, he delivered a stern warning to the volunteers, who were eager to get going. Standing next to a Vermilion Parish Sheriff's Department squad car with a bullhorn in hand, Gautreaux said:

"This is the deal: If you're afraid to see death, don't come. If you're afraid to see a dead body floating in the water, don't come. If you're afraid to be shot at, don't come. If you're not used to the smell of death, don't come with us."

Not one person turned around to leave. Everyone started their vehicles, and hundreds of boat owners left the Acadiana Mall, traveling down I-10 with a police escort, rapidly making their way toward New Orleans – and a life-altering experience that would bring them face to face with human suffering on an unimaginable scale.

Sen. Walter Boasso's S.O.S.: 'My people are dying. Please send help.'

Like State Sen. Nick Gautreaux, State Sen. Walter Boasso of St. Bernard Parish was not content to sit by idly while his fellow Louisianians fought for their very lives.

Sen. Boasso was monitoring the storm at the State's Office of Emergency Preparedness (OEP) in Baton Rouge when the first reports of breaches in the levees came in. He was approached by Captain Brian Clark, a regional supervisor for the Louisiana Department of Wildlife and Fisheries Enforcement (DWFE). He told Boasso that he and DWFE Lt. Col. Keith LaCaze were organizing a search-and-rescue mission of 100 DWFE agents with 60 boats. Clark asked if the senator would come with them, and he readily agreed to join their mission.

Arriving at 2 p.m. at the junction of I-10 and Causeway Boulevard – which had been designated the official rescue staging area – Boasso and the DWFE detail could go no farther south on I-10 due to the floodwaters that stretched as far as they could see. Boasso's plan was to try and reach the St. Claude Avenue

Bridge and get into St. Bernard Parish to survey the damage and rescue any survivors they may encounter.

After a few hours of searching for a safe route, Boasso eventually reached the St. Claude Bridge, but could go no farther. The floodwater had risen so high that the bridge itself was barely above water. Boasso's plan was to travel to the Jackson Barracks, half a mile away, where the National Guard was stationed and where the DWFE kept some of their boats. When Boasso's detail arrived at the St. Claude Bridge they had only 20 boats, as other agents had split up earlier to survey the flood zone.

The DWFE agents with Boasso launched their boats off the side of the St. Claude Bridge, and as soon as their motors were turned on, Boasso heard the forceful voices of desperate people coming from every direction begging for help.

The rescuers were anxious to help as their train of boats motored slowly down St. Claude Avenue. Boasso remembers that moment:

"We didn't make it a block, and I told Brian Clark, 'Let's turn these boats loose.' So we turned everybody loose and told them to go rescue everybody they could rescue. Brian and myself and another agent continued down St. Claude Avenue in our boat, and the people were screaming and hollering for help and shooting flare guns, and saying, 'Please come and get us,' waving towels, hoping we would shine our flashlight on them. All I could tell them again and again was, 'We'll be back at daylight to get you. We'll be back at daylight to get you.' And this went on block after block.

"It was as black as can be. The only lights we had were the broken gas mains that were leaking and had caught on fire. The fires were on top of the water, and the water was still rising. There was no electricity. The city power was out. Dangerous debris was all around us and under the water, like cars and dumpsters. Power lines were down all around us, and floating in the water. You had to move your head to the side to dodge traffic lights and fallen trees. It was slow going."

Traveling deeper into St. Bernard Parish, Clark would occasionally turn off the motor of their boat, and the three men could hear desperate cries for help coming from all directions in the pitch-black darkness.

Boasso's cell phone wouldn't work, so he sent urgent text messages on his Blackberry pleading for help to every friend and associate he could think of throughout the macabre evening's reconnaissance mission.

But Boasso and Clark also knew they had a duty to perform for the people of St. Bernard Parish who needed to be rescued and evacuated to dry land. Boasso had a master plan in mind. After a long, sleepless night, Boasso and Clark aggressively went in search of volunteers to help them assemble what would come to be known as "Camp Katrina," a massive warehouse near the Mississippi River on Chalmette Slip Road. The camp would shelter thousands of evacuees, house tons of emergency supplies, and offer an escape route by ferry across the Mississippi River to dry land at Algiers Point. Setting up the camp would also mean that flood victims scattered throughout the parish could now be brought to one place and quickly evacuated to safety.

Clark recruited volunteers at a local high school, where stranded citizens were crowded on the school's flat, second-story roof. Boasso found more volunteers at a nearby prison that was surrounded by dry land. The work would be done in sweltering south Louisiana heat, with no cool water or tasty food to enjoy during breaks.

The volunteers cleared the warehouse of debris and piles of plywood on pallets, using forklifts and muscle. It was during this cleanup period that Boasso received the text message from his friend and fellow senator, Nick Gautreaux, who was inquiring about the situation in St. Bernard. And it was then that Boasso sent back his chilling reply:

"My people are dying. Please send help."

The rescued flood survivors who were evacuated to safety from Camp Katrina came from every social background and status: doctors, lawyers, waitresses, janitors, teachers, nurses, wealthy and poor.

Because Boasso's cell phone rarely worked, he was forced to send text messages with his Blackberry to enlist the aid of fellow Louisiana government officials to make things happen quickly.

Boasso got help from Ty Bromell, the director of the Governor's Office of Rural Development at the Louisiana Office of Emergency Preparedness (OEP), who recruited buses, drivers and supplies such as ice, water, diapers, generators, medicine, chain saws, and body bags. Buses took evacuees from Algiers Point to Louis Armstrong Airport in Kenner and Belle Chase Airport.

Literally thousands of volunteers donated supplies through Bromell's OEP donation hotline, including the Salvation Army and various non-profit organizations. Hundreds more volunteers helped deliver the supplies.

Louisiana Senator Rob Marionneaux recruited ferries, a barge, and a tugboat – donated by Angus Cooper of Osprey Lines – to move large amounts of supplies downriver from the Port of Greater Baton Rouge to both New Orleans and Camp Katrina.

Boasso also received help from Sam Jones – the governor's liaison to parochial and municipal government – who recruited buses, 18-wheel trucks, and the Cajun Navy volunteers from the Lake Charles area who helped rescue hundreds of residents in St. Bernard Parish and New Orleans.

Lafayette-Abbeville area volunteers make search-and-rescue mission

Wednesday morning at 8 o'clock Gautreaux and his citizen flotilla arrived in New Orleans and *rendezvoused* with Captain

Clark and his Wildlife and Fisheries agents, who had set up headquarters at the Clearview Shopping Center at the junction of I-10 and Clearview Parkway.

According to Gautreaux, the DWFE agents were overwhelmed by the huge number of Cajun Navy volunteers. A long line of trucks and boats of all shapes and sizes stretched for miles, like a cargo train, along I-10.

"We thought we could just go there and start launching boats. But we had to wait. What people didn't understand was that, where they wanted to launch, they would have returned to find their cars underwater. The water was still rising," Gautreaux explains.

Hundreds of volunteers' boats eventually received search-and-rescue assignments that morning from the DWFE. They were led to critical areas throughout the flood zones of New Orleans and St. Bernard Parish through circuitous and hazardous routes. Other volunteers were turned away because their houseboats, party barges, and deep-draft boats were too big or unsafe for a rescue mission. And others simply got tired waiting for an assignment and went home.

Ryan Mathers, a volunteer from Maurice (just south of Lafayette), waited for about four hours. He had borrowed a boat to participate in the search-and-rescue mission – a 14-foot, flat-bottom boat that could seat six passengers. He waited patiently in his truck with his fellow volunteer, Aaron Hoffpauir of Erath, and finally got an assignment from the DWFE. He became part of a 16-boat group of Cajun Navy volunteers who traveled to various staging areas throughout the Ninth Ward. Mathers brought his rescued passengers to a nearby Texaco station, where DWFE agents would load them on buses.

Another volunteer, Deacon Don Leger of St. Barnabas Episcopal Church in Lafayette, embarked on quite a different route than Mathers to find a search-and-rescue assignment. His group of volunteers grew tired of waiting on I-10, and they decided to find a way into the city on their own. The route they chose took them south on Causeway Blvd. to the Huey P. Long Bridge, crossing the Mississippi River into Westwego, then driving south to the Crescent City Connection Bridge, and back across the Mississippi River, then down into New Orleans, where their group was diverted by police, passing by the Convention Center to Harrah's Casino on Canal Street.

When Deacon Leger's group arrived at Harrah's they were told by a Louisiana State Trooper, "We don't need you." Hearing this, some volunteers turned around and went home. But Leger and those who stayed were adamant about finding a mission.

Eventually they found a sympathetic New Orleans police officer who led Leger and 40 boat owners on I-10, over the breached Industrial Canal levee, and into St. Bernard Parish, where they launched their boats from I-10 just north of Chef Menteur Highway.

Before the volunteers launched their boats, the police gave them a few pointers about what they would observe out there in no-man's land.

"The police said, 'Go right out there, and you will hear people, you'll see,'" Leger says. "He said to watch for any movement because some people are in the attics with attic vents, and they'll drop a white cloth or napkin through the vent, so be observant."

At Leger's first stop, he was forced to get waist-deep into the putrid-smelling, murky floodwaters. (Months later, he was still nursing chemical burns on his legs he developed from wading in the contaminated water that was fouled with household chemicals, poisons and raw sewage.)

Leger's impression of the survivors he was saving was that they were extremely desperate.

"People seemed to be in a state of shock and bewilderment. They thought it was only their neighborhood that flooded.

But after riding in the boat for a couple of miles, as far as they could see, they saw devastation. Many had nothing more than a brown paper bag that held what was left of their worldly possessions. People had a forlorn look in their eyes, knowing they'd lost everything," Leger says.

Throughout the day, Leger and his fellow crewman lifted wheelchair-bound elderly survivors into their boat. They had to turn away flood victims swimming toward them in the polluted brown water who tried to grab on to their small, overcrowded craft, begging them with pleas of "one more, please, one more."

Leger's memories of that day include the sight of numerous floating dead animals, swimming snakes, rats, and rabid dogs that had to be pushed away from their boat with an oar.

Toward the end of that hot, tiring day, Leger recalls floating slowly past an apartment complex where a huge black Labrador Retriever was looking out of a second-story window at their passing boat.

"That dog went to the back of the room, and then came running and leaped through the glass window to get out of the apartment," Leger says.

While this amazing animal swam toward their boat, Leger's fellow crewman said, "This dog wants to be saved." When the paddling Lab finally arrived at the side of their boat, the two men hauled the enterprising dog out of the water and gave him a ride to safety.

Even though Leger was told by the New Orleans police to leave pets behind, in defiance he saved a little boy's pet parakeet that had been given to him as a birthday present on the day before the hurricane. He also rescued an elderly woman's newborn puppy by putting it in a shoebox he found at the top of her bedroom closet; he poked air holes into the shoebox cover so the puppy could breathe.

Although Leger was also told to leave dead bodies behind and concentrate on rescuing the living, as an ordained deacon he felt a responsibility to stop for a moment and say a prayer for the deceased when he encountered a dead body.

At the end of his day, with the sunshine rapidly disappearing, Leger decided to hitchhike home to Lafayette, and as soon as he held out his thumb for a ride, a car driven by an LSU student stopped to give the white-collared deacon a lift to Baton Rouge. There he phoned his wife to ask her to come and get him.

Lake Charles area rescuers focus on elderly and infirm

Just a few blocks away from Deacon Don Leger's rescue operation that same Wednesday, the Lake Charles contingent of the Cajun Navy was hard at work rescuing elderly patients, residents and their pets near the Crystal Palace on Chef Menteur Highway in St. Bernard Parish.

By noon their 34-member, 17-boat citizen flotilla had rescued close to 1,000 people. Three rescues occurred at Forest Towers East Apartments, a facility for senior citizens on Lake Forest Boulevard; the Metropolitan Hospice for senior citizen patients on Read Boulevard; and nearby private homes where residents were trapped by the flood. And they would continue their rescue efforts well into the following Sunday afternoon.

The Lake Charles citizen flotilla odyssey began only a day earlier at 6:30 a.m., when Ronny Lovett, owner of R & R Construction in Sulphur, telephoned his friend and New Orleans native, Andy Buisson, to suggest they should get together to help rescue the flood victims they were watching on television that morning. Buisson told Lovett he was already thinking the same thing.

An early riser and former Navy Second Class Petty Officer, Lovett's instinct for volunteerism peaked after he awoke at 3 a.m. and turned on his television to see and hear about the humanitarian disaster unfolding in the Crescent City. Lovett had also helped to assist the victims of Hurricane Andrew in

1992, and has been a public service volunteer continuously throughout his adult life.

Not long after Lovett spoke to Buisson about the idea of doing something to help, he received a phone call from Buisson's wife, Sara Roberts, a certified public accountant in Lake Charles and member of the Superdome Commission. Roberts said she had just received a call from Sam Jones, the governor's liaison to parochial and municipal government, who asked her if she could help find volunteers with boats to rescue stranded flood victims in New Orleans. Jones told Roberts her citizen flotilla volunteers could meet up with Department of Wildlife and Fisheries Enforcement (DWFE) agents in New Orleans at I-10 and Causeway Boulevard.

Hearing this, Lovett immediately set about assembling his navy. With 600 R & R Construction employees to ask for assistance, Lovett promised everyone he contacted hourly wages 24/7 for all volunteers.

"Nobody turned me down," says Lovett, who eventually handpicked only boat owners and experienced boatmen for the mission. He brought along a tool truck and a fuel truck.

In all, Lovett assembled a crew of 17 boats and 34 boatmen from the Lake Charles area and from as far away as Lake Arthur, Ville Platte and Opelousas. Joining them were the boat and supplies of Buisson and Roberts, who led the caravan from Wal-Mart in Jennings toward their New Orleans *rendezvous* with Wildlife and Fisheries agents.

When the Cajun Navy arrived in New Orleans at the designated staging area, I-10 and Causeway Boulevard, they were redirected to Sam's Club on Airline Drive, then to Harrah's Casino on Canal Street, where they spent the night in sleeping bags on the side of the road. They were not far from the Ernest Morial Convention Center, where a huge crowd of hurricane refugees was gathering, hoping to be evacuated soon.

At daybreak Wednesday, the Lake Charles citizen navy was

escorted by New Orleans police to the Crystal Palace on Chef Menteur Highway, where they would launch their vessels and begin rescue operations.

By 2 o'clock Thursday morning, the entire flotilla crew had come to the agreement that they should return to Lake Charles to replenish their food and water supplies, which they had given to the people they rescued.

Early Friday morning Lovett's navy returned to New Orleans to help. Only this time they brought 35 boats and even more boatmen. Buisson returned with the new crew, but Roberts had fallen ill on Wednesday evening and could not participate in the last leg of the mission.

That Friday morning Lovett's replenished crew drove to New Orleans, entering the city from the west bank of the river, anticipating their return to Forest Towers East Apartments and Metropolitan Hospice. They had promised patients and residents of those two facilities that they would return to rescue them. Their plan was thwarted Wednesday evening when they were forced to leave due to their exhausted supplies – and the threat of deadly violence throughout the city that was being reported by the police.

When Lovett's flotilla arrived in Gretna, on the west bank, Friday morning they were asked by the Sheriff's Department to help transport water and emergency supplies from New Orleans to Gretna, to the Jackson Avenue Ferry landing. Lovett's crew complied with the request.

Then, after having accomplished that task, Lovett's employees were asked to clear trees and debris from strategic Gretna area roads with bulldozers. These clearing efforts took the rest of the day Friday, forcing Lovett's crew to bed down in their trucks at Harrah's Casino that evening.

At dawn Saturday Lovett's citizen flotilla headed back to Forest Towers East Apartments to continue their rescue efforts. They were surprised to discover the residents they had to leave behind Wednesday evening had yet to be evacuated. Saturday's rescue operation would take half a day.

On Sunday Lovett's crew returned to Metropolitan Hospice and once again found familiar faces were still there and clinging to life. One particular hospice resident was an African-American chaplain who would not leave Wednesday evening with Lovett's crew without also bringing the six elderly bedridden white female patients for whom he was caring. On Sunday afternoon, when the Cajun Navy returned, the chaplain was still there but only two of the women were still alive.

Before the chaplain would allow the Cajun Navy to take the two remaining women, Lovett had to guarantee they would not be stranded on the side of the road, waiting for hours in the hot sun for evacuation from the Crystal Palace staging area.

So, with this in mind, Lovett returned to Crystal Palace with a boatload of evacuees, thinking of a way to further evacuate the chaplain's patients. After he arrived, as luck would have it, he saw a Navy truck traveling toward him on Chef Menteur Highway. Lovett flagged down the military vehicle. After the Navy personnel listened to his story about the chaplain and his two friends, the driver agreed to wait at Crystal Palace for Lovett to return with the chaplain and the women, who were then taken to a medical facility in Baton Rouge.

That Sunday afternoon, as rescue operations were winding down, Lovett and his hard-working construction company employees packed up their gear, hitched their boats to their trucks, and left New Orleans. They had saved hundreds of lives.

Little did they know that their selfless actions would eventually become legendary – one of the bright lights in a dark, sad tale.

Eyewitness to a nightmare

State Rep. Donald Cravins Jr., one of Opelousas's reserve police officers, went to New Orleans to help out after Hurricane Katrina. He witnessed some terrible things that he won't soon forget.

By Jefferson Hennessy

In the wake of Hurricane Katrina, State Representative Donald Cravins Jr., an Opelousas attorney and reserve police officer, answered a call that went out to local law-enforcement agencies requesting help from police volunteers to assist a Sheriff's Task Force in New Orleans.

Early Tuesday morning, August 30, Cravins set out for Gonzales to join the task force at the Lamar-Dixon Expo Center. He was assigned to assist in the evacuation of prisoners from New Orleans. Over the next 48 hours he witnessed tragedy on a massive scale.

He recalls those disheartening days.

"On Tuesday, my first day, we were stationed at the LaPlace exit directing traffic on I-10 that was trying to get to the city of New Orleans or Jefferson Parish, making sure that only emergency personnel got through. As the morning progressed we learned that the water level was rising.

"The second day, Wednesday, we moved prisoners on buses from the Orleans Parish prisons.... They had no food, they had no water for several days. It was so flooded on I-10, directly across from the prison, we had to airboat the prisoners from the jail to I-10 and corral them on a small stretch of highway.

"While we were evacuating prisoners by boat, thousands of them, the incident that has captured my memory is the sight of people emerging from the flooded waters walking toward us carrying bodies with them in makeshift boats, carrying ailing loved ones with them, carrying children with them. And those people had been walking for a day and a half. They had not had any food, had not had any water. And the floodwater was full of oil and gas and bodies. I'll always remember those people in the distance coming out from the water toward us. It was like something you would see in a horror movie.

"We moved prisoners to the side so we could make room for these people. They were trying to get to the Superdome. They were lost, literally lost. And I saw only one New Orleans deputy that day.

"I also saw many people stranded on I-10 across from the Superdome. They were stranded there and couldn't get across the floodwater. They had been living on that hot concrete for days with no water and no food – and nobody was dropping any food to them. We can do that in every other country but America. There were some helicopters flying around, but I didn't know what they were doing.

"On Thursday I get home and I've had enough. Someone's been shooting at police officers on Wednesday. There were reports that they'd killed several officers. A sheriff had called our unit in Gonzales on Wednesday saying, 'My men are taking fire! My men are taking fire on Elysian Fields! They are escorting firemen. They're taking fire! We need backup!'

"It was frustrating as hell, because it took an hour to get from Gonzales to New Orleans, and we had no communications in the city. Our radios couldn't communicate with anyone else's radio but the Opelousas police.

"But I went back with Lt. Bruce Alsandor, who said he was going back to rescue the grandchildren of a former mayor of Opelousas. I told him, 'You can't go alone.' So I rode with Bruce in a police squad car to New Orleans, and we drove across the West Bank Bridge onto Convention Avenue.

"What I saw on Convention Avenue was the worst thing

I've ever seen in my entire life. They had let everybody out of the Convention Center, and people were literally dying on the street. They had no food. It was so hot outside. They had finally begun to bring them some water. We had to drive through these miserable, miserable people with law enforcement on one side, guns blazing. These people had been in the Convention Center for three or four days. Bodies, litter everywhere. It was like a crowd scene you would see in India, not in the United States.

"But we made it through and out again with the mayor's grandkids and their mother. And I remember thinking, *This is the greatest thing I've ever done in my life.*

"Then, on the way home I heard that a bus filled with evacuees had crashed near Opelousas. Automatically, every good thought drained out of me."

Dr. Antoine Keller practices medicine in a makeshift clinic in the Superdome

By Jefferson Hennessy

Early on Wednesday morning August 31, 2005, Lafayette cardiovascular surgeon, Dr. Antoine Keller was contacted by Ross and Remi Judice of Acadian Ambulance Service in Lafayette and asked if he would volunteer to travel with them to New Orleans to treat victims of Hurricane Katrina. The mission: to help care for what they estimated to be more than 20,000 people in the Superdome without access to medical assistance.

Without hesitation, Dr. Keller, a native of New Orleans, agreed to join them and a few other physicians who would make the flight that day. They would be the first physicians to arrive at the Superdome. They were stunned by what they saw.

Dr. Keller recalls the chaotic events of that day.

"We landed on the parking deck of the Superdome and were immediately greeted by thousands of people who were stranded, didn't have anywhere to go, or the means to get there. After we landed we realized we didn't have much in the way of supplies to treat the people who were sick. That was the second blow that really let us know what we were in for.

"The illnesses we treated were people with diabetes who hadn't had their insulin in days, people with renal failure on hemodialysis who hadn't been dialyzed in days, people suffering from heat stroke. The Superdome had no air conditioning, or electricity, no lights, no working toilets for two days at that point. Having all those people in a closed space very close together made the heat almost unbearable.

"We set up a small clinic inside the Superdome in one of the small offices – which was really no more than a closet. We had some basic lifesaving tools like a defibrillator and some basic IV setups and IV fluids that were diminishing by the moment. We had no way to get supplies in or out other than by the grace of Acadian Ambulance Service. We phoned on our satellite phone to all the hospitals in Lafayette and asked them to send whatever they could. Throughout the course of the day we managed to make do, seeing hundreds of patients and trying to evacuate the most significantly ill patients as soon as possible. That effort was hampered in part by the fact that we could only get four or five patients out on every helicopter.

"Our clinic in the Superdome quickly became a very hostile environment because people were desperate. They had not had adequate food or water in days. They had unsanitary conditions among a lot of very sick people, and a lot of children. So we had to move our clinic outside because it was a matter of safety for us. People were fighting each other, and threatening the physicians, and yelling expletives about the mayor and the governor and all the other people who might have been partially responsible for them being there.

"Throughout the day the most disturbing thing was there didn't seem to be any action with regard to a plan about getting people to places that were a little bit more comfortable, or where we were to send patients if we were about to begin evacuation. Without the help of Acadian Ambulance at the Superdome those first several days those patients would never have gotten the medical care they needed, or the organization to get them out to a place where they could be cared for.

"We stayed until early Thursday morning, at which time the officials in charge mandated that we had to leave because the conditions had deteriorated to being so unsafe that we were at risk of being hurt or gravely injured. So, we left."

The heroic evacuation of Touro Infirmary

When emergency generators failed following Hurricane Katrina, Dr. Victor Tedesco and his staff had to act quickly to save their 250 patients. Helicopters, buses, minibuses and a SWAT team all contributed to this daring rescue.

By Jefferson Hennessy

Monday, August 29, 2005. In the early evening hours after Hurricane Katrina ravaged New Orleans with torrential rain and Category 3 winds, the medical staff at Touro Infirmary believed they had survived the massive storm without incurring much damage to their venerable hospital. But Monday afternoon some of the hospital's backup emergency generators began to fail, and that meant trouble for everyone in the facility.

For the next three days conditions at Touro Infirmary would deteriorate, initiating an unprecedented scene of heroic life-and-death efforts to evacuate the hospital's frailest and life-support-dependent patients.

As president of the medical staff, cardiac and vascular surgeon Dr. Victor E. Tedesco IV found himself in the middle of a humanitarian calamity that would test his physical endurance and organizational skills far beyond what he assumed was his capacity.

Days before Katrina arrived, Dr. Tedesco and his staff made all the preparations they thought necessary to sustain the hospital's electrical power and communications network.

Many of the staff members even brought their family members and pets to Touro to ride out the storm, including Dr. Tedesco, who brought his wife, their two children, and the family dog and cat.

"We were prepared for the storm," Dr. Tedesco says. "We put our disaster plan in effect on Saturday. We trucked in extra fuel for our generators, and we had food and water supplies, plus two shifts of medical staff. We had five generators, but two of the most important ones failed."

One generator that failed caused the bed tower to lose power; the other that failed powered the chillers that provided air to the entire building. With this, the infirmary became an extremely hot, windless death trap for Touro's most critical patients. With very little light, no air conditioning, no running water, and disabled elevators for the ten-story building, Dr. Tedesco and his staff knew they had to begin evacuating their 250 patients.

But before the evacuation could begin, Dr. Tedesco and his staff had to solve a big problem: They could not find a telephone that worked, including the staff's cell phones.

*   *   *   *   *

Tuesday, August 30, 2005. In the early morning hours on Tuesday a staff member made an astounding discovery. In one of the hospital's emergency room waiting areas, she found a pay phone with a dial tone.

For the next 48 hours, Dr. Tedesco and his staff pumped quarters into that pay phone in a desperate effort to make contact with the outside world, and the effort succeeded.

The first evacuees were the hospital's 13 newborn babies on life-support systems and in critical condition. Air Med helicopters arrived quickly to transport the little patients to safety.

But all day Tuesday and into the evening, Dr. Tedesco could not locate a medical facility that could accept his adult patients. There was just no room in the inn. Nor could he locate anyone to evacuate these patients.

Though Touro had lost much of its generator power, there

was enough juice to run a few televisions that revealed to everyone in the facility the extent of the great deluge and the humanitarian crisis that was New Orleans.

*   *   *   *   *

Wednesday, August 31, 2005. In the afternoon, one of the hospital administrators got in touch with Acadian Ambulance Air Med Service to request the assistance of helicopters to evacuate Touro's adult patients.

During the day Dr. Tedesco tried to contact his father, Dr. Victor E. Tedesco III, the coroner of Terrebonne Parish, in Houma. Although he couldn't reach his father, he did locate a safe medical facility for some of his patients – a makeshift hospital set up in the Houma Civic Center.

"I got in touch with the Terrebonne General Medical Center in Houma while trying to get in touch with my father, the coroner of Terrebonne Parish," Dr. Tedesco says. "Communications were spotty, but I got through to an operator there and talked to the nursing supervisor. They found room for our ambulatory patients at the Houma Civic Center, where they had set up an evacuation center. They took 12 in-patients and about 30 of our ambulatory patients.... We also evacuated our 25 psychiatric patients to Alexandria. But by Wednesday afternoon the van drivers were too scared to come back into New Orleans because looting and shooting stories were rampant."

By Wednesday, Dr. Tedesco and his staff had been trudging up and down 10 flights of stairs at Touro for two days, administering food, medicine and comfort to their patients who were trapped in a hotbox. One hundred of these patients were what Dr. Tedesco describes as "the sickest of the sick" – elderly, bedridden, and dependent upon life-support systems.

When Acadian Ambulance Air Med Service arrived that afternoon, a flight paramedic with Acadian gave Dr. Tedesco good news and bad news. The paramedic said Acadian Ambulance would work through the night to try to evacuate all of Touro's remaining patients. That was the good news. But in order to evacuate, the hospital staff would first have to bring "the sickest of the sick" to the roof of a parking garage next door, where a helipad was located.

As darkness fell, Dr. Tedesco and his staff dutifully began carrying their last 100 patients down the hospital's stairs to the third floor, then to the parking garage by way of a cross-bridge that linked the two buildings. After two Acadian Ambulance choppers had arrived and departed, the helicopters stopped coming.

In spite of this disheartening development, Dr. Tedesco and his staff continued to pick up patients in their arms and carry them to the roof of the parking garage. After a few hours of moving patients and waiting for choppers, Dr. Tedesco received word that Acadian Ambulance's Air Med helicopters had been diverted to another medical facility whose patients were in even more dire circumstances than those at Touro. It seemed that no more helicopters would be coming to Touro.

Because it was cooler outdoors than inside the hospital, Dr. Tedesco decided his team would administer care to their patients on the roof of the parking garage while continuing to try to establish contact with transportation and medical facility resources.

*　*　*　*　*

Thursday, September 1, 2005. Early Thursday morning Dr. Tedesco was exhausted and deeply concerned about his patients and his staff, so he tried another tactic in an effort to resolve the crisis.

"I called my dad. I said, 'Dad, I'm in trouble. I need some help,'" Dr. Tedesco recalls.

As coroner of Terrebonne Parish, Dr. Tedesco's father had connections to powerful resources beyond his son's reach. When the younger Dr. Tedesco finally made contact with his father and related the story of his extraordinary troubles, his father told him, "Okay, I'll call you right back."

Within a few minutes Dr. Tedesco received a call – on the pay phone in the ER waiting area – from Jerry Larpenter, the sheriff of Terrebonne Parish, who said he was on his way to Touro Infirmary with 10 minibuses and a SWAT team.

"I was relieved to hear that news," Dr. Tedesco says.

Before Sheriff Larpenter arrived, two more unexpected events occurred.

At about 10 a.m. the CEO of Touro managed to get in touch with an ABC News camera crew. Soon after, journalist Bob Woodruff was flown to Touro to interview Dr. Tedesco in a live broadcast – and show the world the desperate condition of the hospital's patients. Not long after Woodruff's story was shown on television, help was on the way.

"Miraculously, helicopters began to show up at Touro to evacuate our patients," Dr. Tedesco reports.

Then at noon, New Orleans police arrived to tell Dr. Tedesco they had lost control of the city. The police insisted that Dr. Tedesco and the entire staff of Touro "will be evacuated immediately," explaining that their lives may be in danger.

"We're not leaving until we get these patients out of here," Dr. Tedesco told the police.

But the police insisted.

"Two Greyhound buses were used to evacuate staff members, ancillary support people, and some medical personnel. We were now left with 13 doctors, 20 nurses and a few administrators to care for the 80 or 90 patients still on top of the parking garage," Dr. Tedesco explains.

As the last of the evacuating staff were being driven away from Touro, Sheriff Larpenter, 10 minibuses, and a SWAT team arrived to evacuate the remaining critically ill patients, who were by now in desperate need of medical attention.

Larpenter's heavily armed SWAT team encircled Touro Infirmary for two city blocks while Dr. Tedesco and his staff quickly loaded their remaining patients on buses that would take them to Houma and Lafayette for emergency medical care. Meanwhile, helicopters were still arriving spontaneously and departing with patients from the parking garage roof.

"The scene was chaotic," Dr. Tedesco recalls. "It looked like the evacuation of Saigon."

Just when Dr. Tedesco's ordeal appeared to be nearing its end, New Orleans police returned to say they had received a report that a hostage was being held at gunpoint on the seventh floor of Touro Infirmary. Dr. Tedesco volunteered to go up to the seventh floor in the dark hospital with six SWAT team agents with flashlights mounted on their guns. The SWAT team led the way, Dr. Tedesco was behind them, and two National Guardsmen brought up the rear. The agents broke open doors and shouted "Clear!" then moved on to the next room and the next. They searched every room on the seventh floor, but no hostage situation was found.

In addition to evacuating all the remaining patients from Touro, Sheriff Larpenter's team used a few minibuses to help evacuate patients from an acute long-term care facility next door to the hospital.

The evacuation caravan leaving Touro Infirmary was a long one, with New Orleans residents spontaneously joining the SWAT team escort out of the city and across the Crescent City Connection bridge into Gretna, and beyond.

"We had two miles of cars coming out of New Orleans," Sheriff Larpenter says.

With the hospital now evacuated completely, Dr. Tedesco went to check on the condition of his house in Gretna. When he arrived he found that little damage was done. With no running water in the house, he still couldn't take a bath to wash off four days of hard work.

Tired but very relieved, he cleaned out his refrigerator, then drove to his father's house in Houma with a whale of a story to tell. He telephoned his wife and two children to find out how they were doing in New Iberia, where he had sent them Tuesday morning in the family truck.

"I feel I was fortunate to be able to witness some of the best of humanity," Dr. Tedesco says, "with everyone trying to help these patients who were totally helpless and reliant upon us. Some of the worst of humanity was going on all around us, but that's not what I saw. It was an unbelievable experience – but I don't ever want to do it again."

His determination and tireless efforts to evacuate every patient from the hospital earned him the 2006 Judah Touro Society Award "in recognition of an individual's contribution to the welfare of Touro Infirmary."

Because Hurricane Katrina wiped out his New Orleans business, Dr. Tedesco is now practicing heart surgery in Lafayette, where he and his family have found a new home.

Dealing with a new reality at West Jefferson Medical Center

By Patricia Gannon

Holly Broussard is a night shift nurse at West Jefferson Medical Center in Marrero, across the river from New Orleans. She's used to the dark and dismal side of life that one sees only on long, hot nights in the city.

But, like many, she was unprepared for reality when Katrina checked in one fateful day in August.

As the storm roared ashore 20 miles east of New Orleans, the hospital lost its electricity at dawn and was down for an hour before emergency generators kicked in. While hospital personnel manned flashlights in the corridors, on Broussard's fourth floor watch there was more to fear than the dark.

"The wind was bad," she says. "Glass was shattering in some rooms as we scrambled to move patients into the hallway, including those with oxygen tanks. It was a stressful, get-it-now situation."

But not as stressful as it would become once the storm had passed.

Hospital CEO Gary Muller made the first of several futile calls to FEMA (Federal Emergency Management Agency) and was told he was "being evaluated," Broussard reports.

"We were one of three hospitals in the city running at maximum capacity. Water became very difficult," she explains.

Meanwhile, Muller devised an emergency rationing system for the 470-bed facility.

"Each patient had a washbasin of water, that was all, for

drinking and bathing," Broussard says. "We dipped it out with a sterile cup. We were also extremely low on food. It was very scary."

As hospital executives begged FEMA by phone for an additional generator, the temperature within the hospital rose beyond 95 degrees. Linens became scarce and patients with soiled bedding were simply given new pads. When the water shortage grew more acute, patients were cleaned with alcohol. Nurses began cutting their uniforms and ripping off sleeves.

"Our boss told us, 'Do what you have to do, just wear your badge,'" Broussard says.

For a few hours, nurses made cold compresses to put in the back-up freezer for patients with breathing difficulties.

"Medicine refrigerators were running on emergency power; patients were dripping with sweat. We took medical cups, filled them with juice and made small popsicles in the medicine refrigerator. Each patient was allowed to have one every six hours. One man cried when I handed him one," she recalls.

Broussard was on duty for seven 12-hour shifts in a row. She spent some of that time sleeping on the hospital floor. When Muller learned of the situation, he ordered stretchers brought in for nurses to sleep on.

"He said we were the backbone of the hospital and would not sleep on the floor," Broussard recalls, her voice breaking with emotion.

Temperatures soared outside as well. Looters fired on a West Jefferson ambulance, prompting the military to surround the facility and lock it down. National guardsmen and police allowed no one to come or go.

"You couldn't get in unless you were critical," Broussard says. "We were already filled to capacity and had run out of food and water."

Hope for emergency aid dwindled in the stifling heat, and hospital supervisors devised further measures for survival.

"Our boss said he'd be damned if his staff and patients would go hungry," Broussard recalls.

With the aid of East Jefferson police, a neighboring Wal-Mart was informed that if its doors weren't opened voluntarily, they'd be broken. The store acquiesced, and directors of nursing procured provisions, pausing long enough to take slippers for nurses whose feet had blistered from excessive perspiration and overwork.

"When you have bosses and executives who care, it really makes a difference," she says. "I've talked to nurses since, and there were many walkouts at other places."

Broussard credits the courage and leadership of hospital administrators Gary Muller and Cathy Ruppert for the fact that, despite the ordeal, not a single patient was lost.

Newlyweds lose their home in the flood

By Melanie Melancon

For Richard and Julie Laurent, both 23 years old, Houma was their second home, a place visited on the weekends and for holidays and family celebrations. But after the floodwaters from Hurricane Katrina destroyed their Lakeview home in New Orleans, the newlyweds began calling Houma their "temporary, maybe permanent residence."

"I have nothing from my childhood left," Richard says, explaining that his parents' home in Meraux, in St. Bernard Parish, was completely destroyed in the hurricane. "My parents have nothing left."

The Laurents have decided not to return to their historic home off of Canal Street in New Orleans. Six feet of water inundated their neighborhood, making all of their property, including Julie's car, unsalvageable.

"I don't want to go back because I know it will never be the same," Richard says.

Julie agrees and adds with a solemn smile, "We lived in a perfect place. If I had to live there the rest of my life, I would have been happy."

Lakeview was a blend of artists, young professionals, families and elderly people who spent their entire lives there. But despite its diversity it was a close-knit community whose residents watched over each other and, at times, celebrated together.

The hours leading up to the evacuation happened fast. The Laurents were babysitting their twin nieces that weekend. When the couple woke up Saturday morning and saw the change in Katrina's projected path, they packed hurriedly and left New Orleans.

They took only one suitcase of clothes, their wedding album and a laptop computer. The tin of photos that marked Julie's entire life was left behind in the rush. The pictures were ruined in the flood.

"All we were thinking about was getting the twins out of the city before the traffic began backing up. There was no time to contemplate," she explains.

After reuniting the twins with their parents in Houma, Julie and Richard drove 11 hours to Houston, where they stayed glued to the hotel's television, watching Katrina pound south Louisiana and Mississippi.

They returned to Houma Monday afternoon, thinking, hoping, New Orleans was spared the worst. But that wasn't the case.

"The most heartbreaking thing about our situation is that we were beginning to gain financial freedom. We were not struggling. And we really only had a month to enjoy that," Julie says.

The couple celebrated their first anniversary in June 2005. It was a difficult first year financially, as Julie was finishing her last year at the University of New Orleans. Richard was a recent graduate in psychology, and their situation improved when he landed a job as a research coordinator for the Department of Psychology at LSU Health Sciences in New Orleans. In August Julie had been promoted to academic coordinator for the Department of Pharmacology at LSU Health Sciences, where she had worked as an office assistant while in college. Life was good.

Now, the couple is uncertain about the future. Julie commutes to Baton Rouge, where Health Sciences has relocated temporarily, to work a couple of days a week. And Richard's plans to apply to graduate school had to be put on hold.

But despite the disorder in their lives, the couple remains optimistic.

"Our life together has just begun. We are young," Julie says. "And we have our family helping us in every way possible."

In Search of the Soul of New Orleans

I awake each morning
to the sounds of
cries, looks, screams.

Are they from
the city, the people,
the soul of New Orleans
aching to be free to return home?

Or are they from my pain,
my confusion, my soul
aching to be free to return home?

The faces, the arms, the hands
Reaching for someone to touch them
Reaching for someone to touch.

Who is listening?
Who is caring?
Who wants to touch dirty
faces, arms, hands?

There is war in Iraq
There is death in our city
There is the excursion into unreality
  that we will return the same.
Yet the dirty faces, arms, hands
Invite us not –
  to ignore life as it is
  to deny the dirty, the grubby,
  the hurting
But invite us –
  to have the strength to deal with life
  as it is.

Where is your soul, oh City?
Where can I find you?
Let me touch your face,
arms, hands

Show me your soul – lead the way
Teach me how to Second Line
  my way into new life,
A new life that can free the cries,
  the looks, the screams
A Second Line that embraces
  all those who want to join in.

Oh, soul of New Orleans
Let us dance with new partners
Let us drink with new wine
Let us hear your music
  with new ears.

Oh, soul of New Orleans change us
Like the mighty River
  flowing through you
Flow through us
Let us bring the silt
  of our experiences
  into the hearts
  of those around us.

Who is listening?
Who is caring?
Who wants to touch the dirty
  faces, arms, hands?

Your people, newly cultivated,
  changed
Aching to return home!

– Mary Beth Mouch, M.S.C.

– Photo courtesy of NASA/Jeff Schmaltz, MODIS Land Rapid Response Team

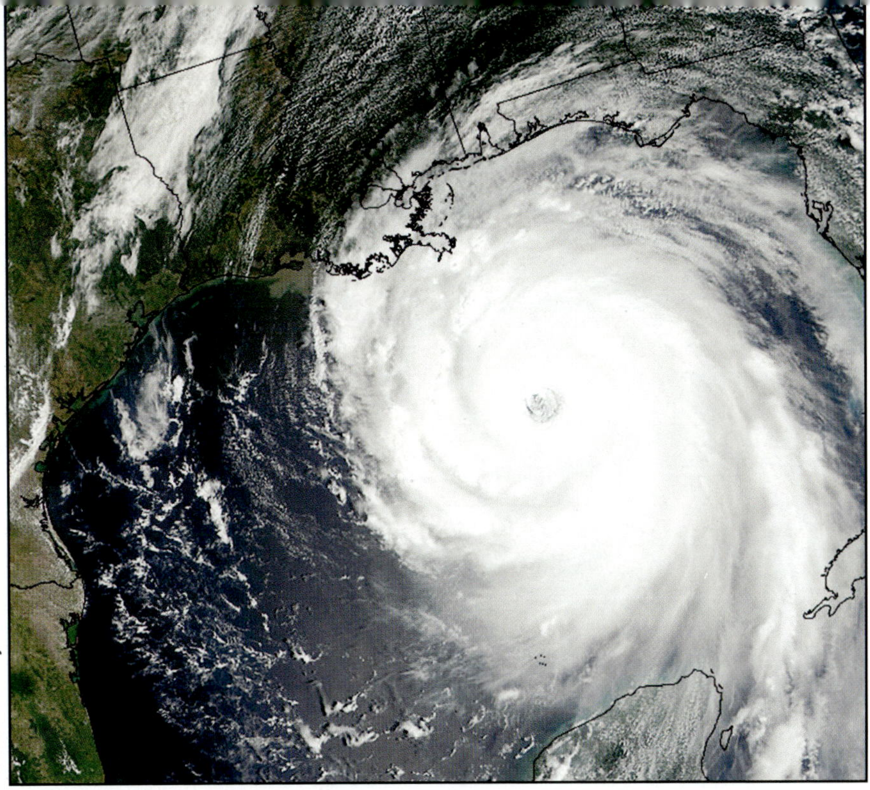

The exodus from New Orleans for Hurricane Katrina was one of the most thorough evacuations in U.S. history, with approximately 80 percent of the population leaving the metropolitan area. Still, tens of thousands stayed behind for various reasons. **Above:** *The massive and powerful storm heads for the southeastern Louisiana coast.* **Below:** *On Sunday August 28, 2005, the day before the storm hit, thousands of people stood in line waiting to take refuge in the Superdome.*

– Photo by Ray Bias, courtesy of Acadian Ambulance Service

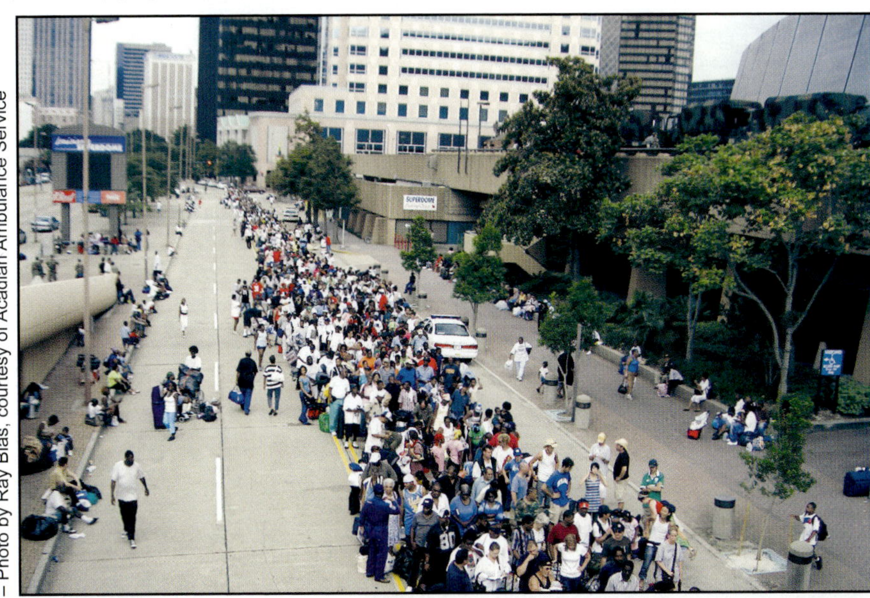

– Photo by John McCusker, *The Times-Picayune*

Hurricane Katrina's powerful storm surge caused the failure of levees and seawalls in and around New Orleans, inundating the city and contributing to the worst natural disaster in U.S. history. **Above:** *Water pours into a residential area through one of several breaches in the levee system.* **Facing page:** *The London Avenue Canal's seawall was breached by the high water, and the neighborhood it was protecting was flooded.*

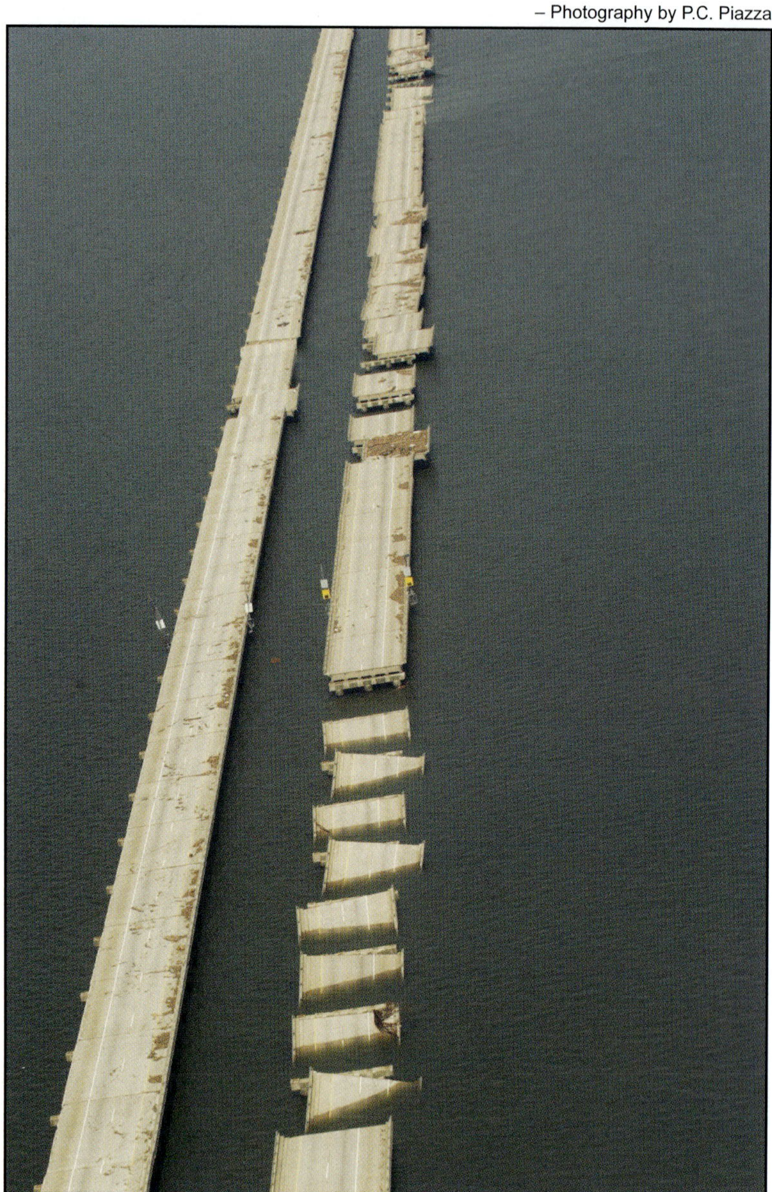

Numerous sections of the bridge over Lake Pontchartrain collapsed due to Hurricane Katrina's storm surge.

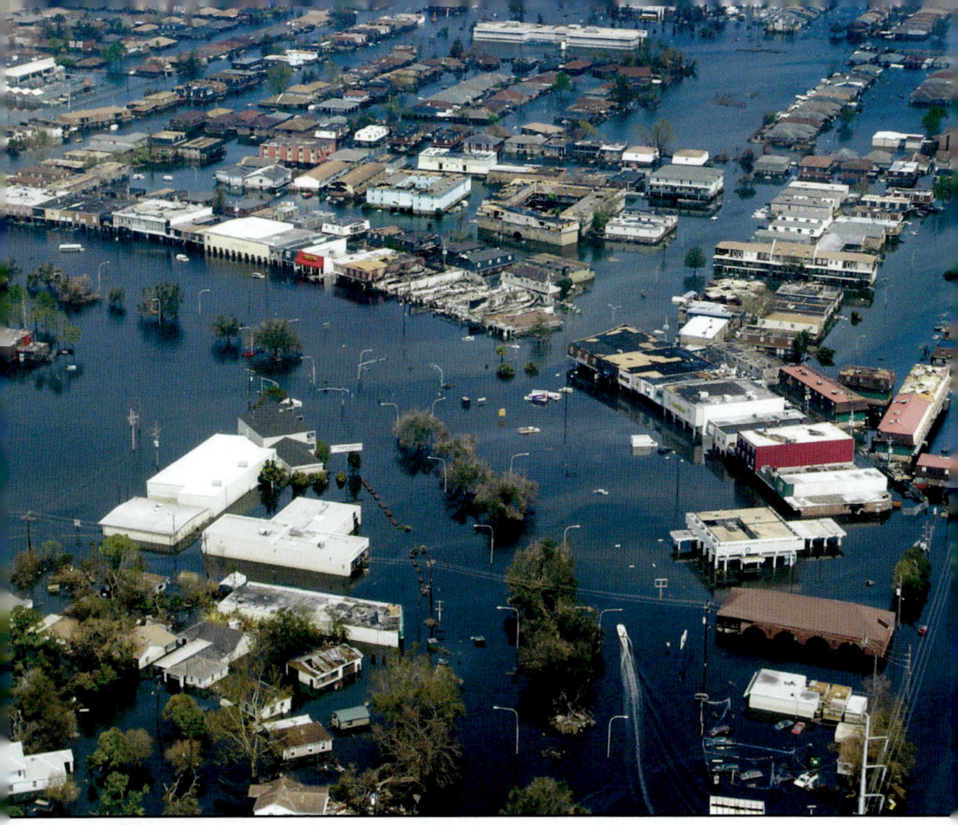

Some 75 to 80 percent of New Orleans was flooded as a result of Hurricane Katrina's powerful storm surge. The flood left the city underwater for days; it was a foot or two in some places, 5 or 6 feet deep in others, and 20 feet deep in others.

– Photos by Ray Bias, courtesy of Acadian Ambulance Service

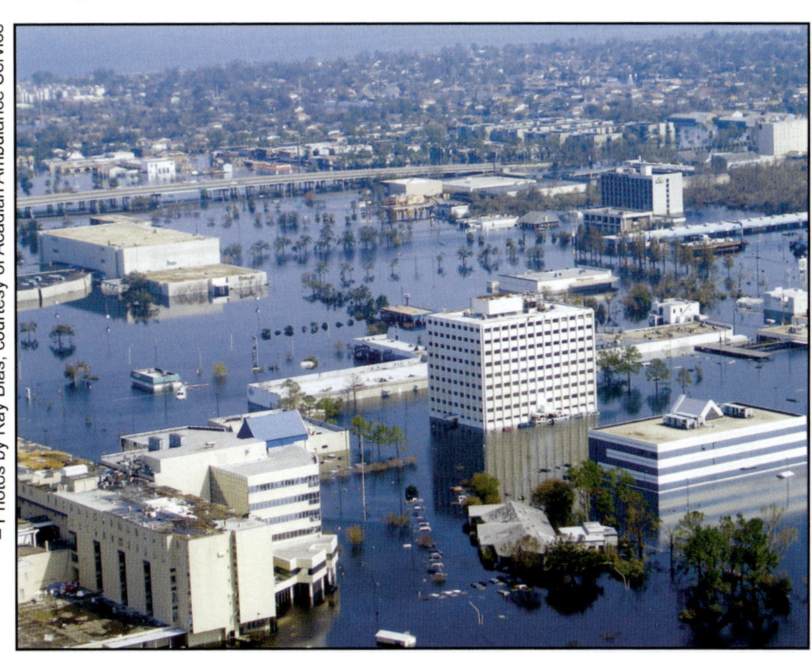

– Photos courtesy of the U.S. Army Corps of Engine

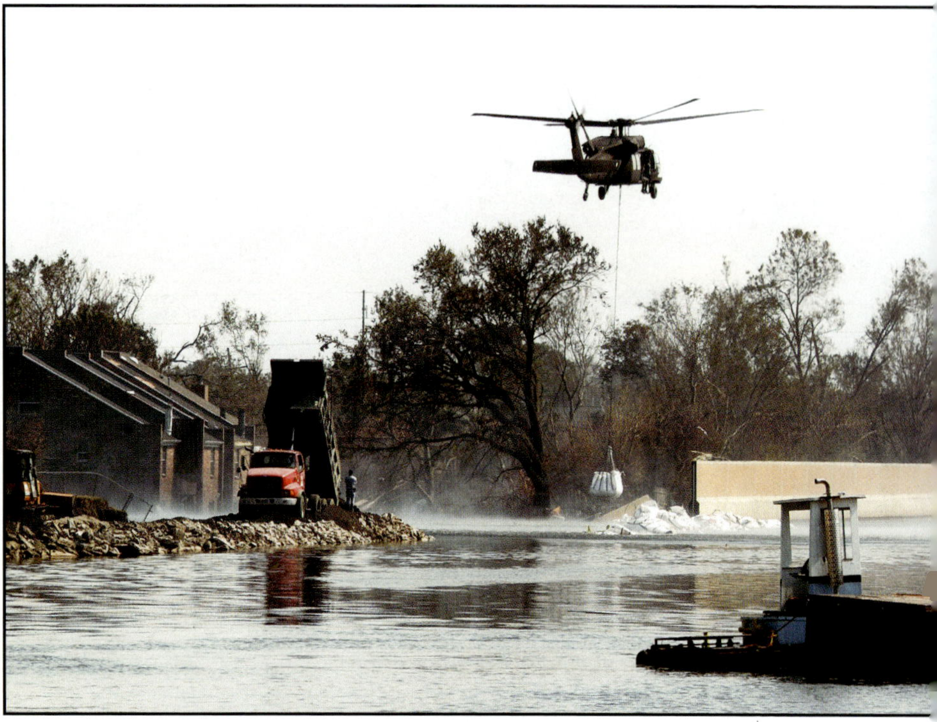

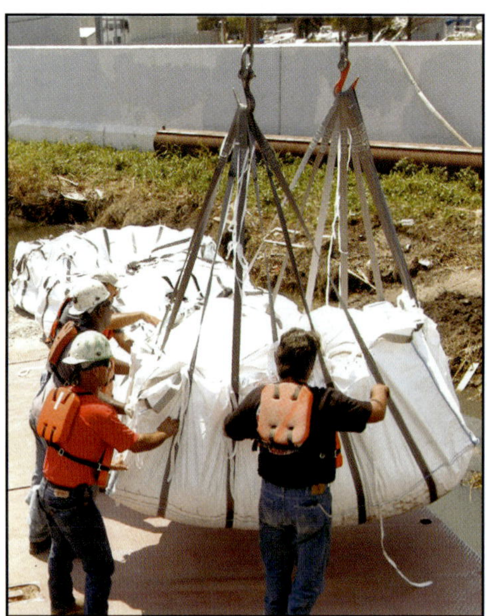

A U.S. Army Corps of Engineers helicopter lowers 3,000-pound sandbags called "supersacks" into place to form a type of dam. The dam temporarily holds back water so that broken seawalls – designed to protect New Orleans from flooding – can be repaired or replaced.

Lt. General Russel Honoré and his troops played a major role in the rescue and evacuation of New Orleans citizens after Hurricane Katrina. Under his command were 20,000 troops and 200 helicopters, as well as 20 ships and a large number of vehicles. **Above:** At the New Orleans airport, Honoré consults with Major General Bill Caldwell of the 82nd Airborne, the U.S. military's premier rapid-deployment force.
Below: At the New Orleans Convention Center, Honoré collaborates with Lt. Col. Jacques Thibodeaux of the Louisiana National Guard regarding evacuation of storm victims from the center.

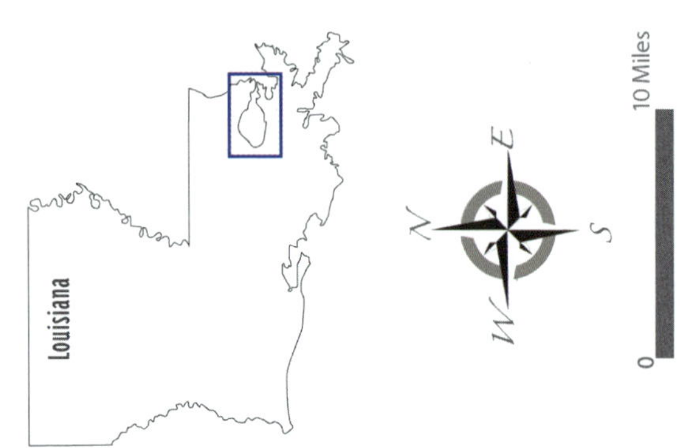

GREATER NEW ORLEANS AREA
Mississippi
Lake Catherine
Lake Borgne
St. Bernard Parish
Pearl River
Slidell
St. Tammany Parish
Intracoastal Waterway
Chalmette
Orleans Parish
Plaquemines Parish
Mandeville
Gretna
Belle Chasse
New Orleans
Jefferson Parish
Covington
Pontchartrain Causeway
Metairie
Westwego
Kenner
12
St. Charles Parish
90
St. John Parish
Lake Pontchartrain
Norco
10
La Place
51
Hammond
Ponchatoula
Lake Maurepas
Mississippi River
Louisiana
N
E
S
W
10 Miles
0

– Illustrated by Don Fields, Lafayette, La.

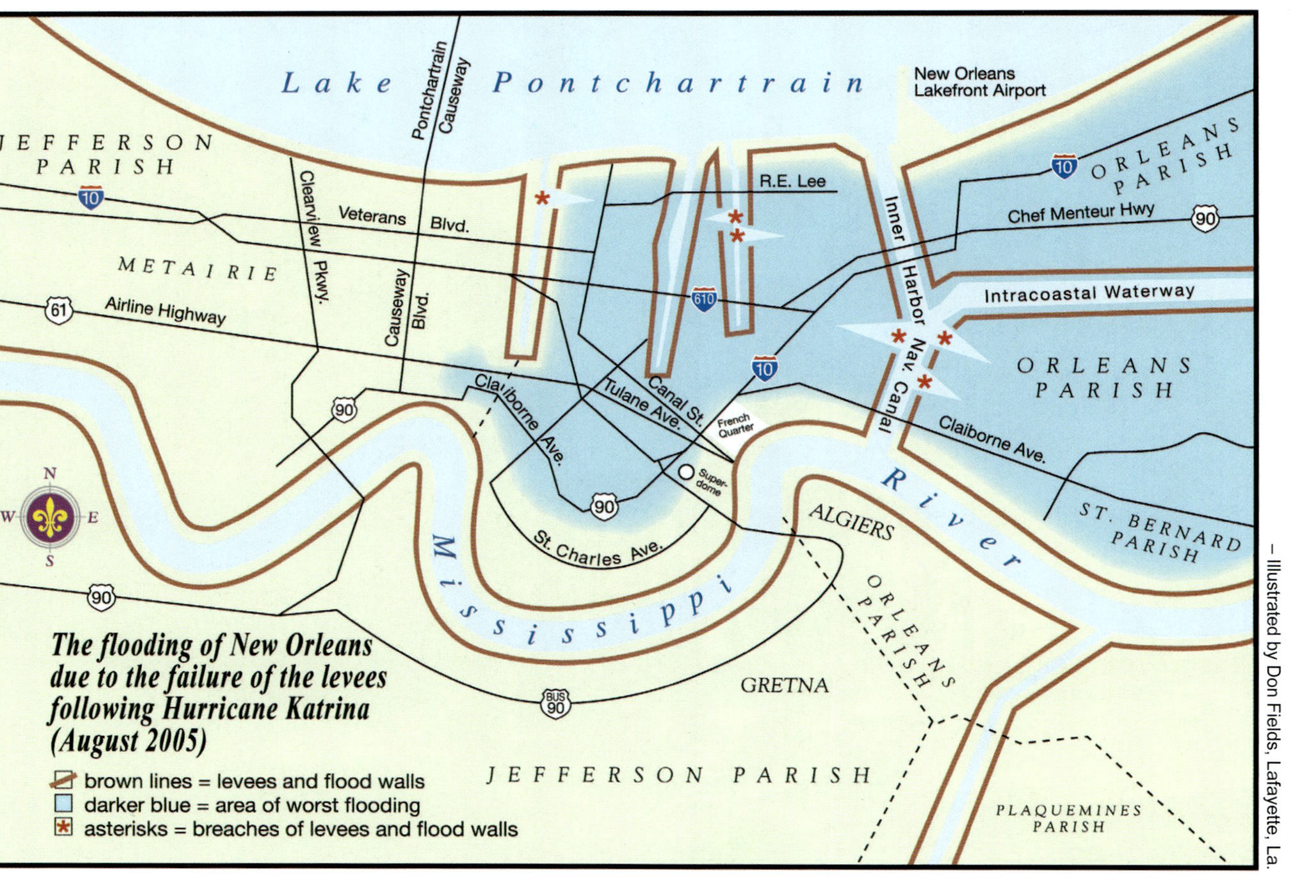

The flooding of New Orleans due to the failure of the levees following Hurricane Katrina *(August 2005)*

– Photo courtesy of Acadian Ambulance and Air Med Services

Tens of thousands of people waited for buses outside the Superdome and the New Orleans Convention Center after Hurricane Katrina. **Above:** *Tanisha Belvin, age 5, holds the hand of fellow storm victim Nita LaGarde, 89, as they are evacuated from the Convention Center on Sept. 3, 2005. This photo was published on front pages of newspapers around the nation, endearing the pair to many Americans.* **Facing page:** *Evacuees at the Superdome wait for a ride to out-of-town shelters or, in many cases, to hospitals for medical treatment.*

Critically ill patients are evacuated from the Superdome in an Army truck as the vehicle moves through floodwaters in downtown New Orleans.

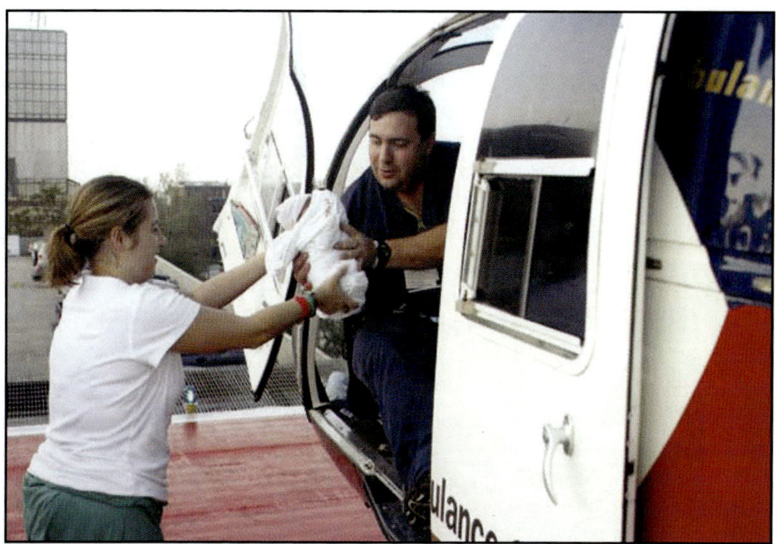

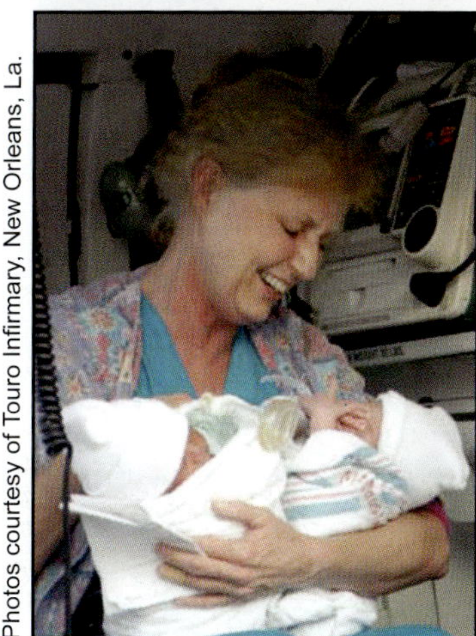

Medical personnel from Women's & Children's Hospital of Lafayette help evacuate newborns from Touro Infirmary following Hurricane Katrina in the summer of 2005. The tiny patients were transported out of New Orleans to Lafayette on Air Med helicopters. **Top:** *Guiliana Larocca, OB tech with Touro, hands a baby to Coby Johnson, CRTT, of Women's & Children's.* **Above, left:** *Cherryl Friday, RNC, of Women's & Children's welcomes her two charges.* **Above, right:** *Coby Johnson secures two infants on the helicopter.*

Among those who helped rescue New Orleans area residents following Hurricane Katrina were members of "The Cajun Navy," made up of groups from the Lafayette and Lake Charles areas. **Above:** *State Sen. Nick Gautreaux of Abbeville (in green shirt) and Sgt. Michael Murray of the Louisiana Department of Wildlife and Fisheries (with shotgun) lead a team of volunteers who safely evacuated the remaining seminarians, priests and staff from Notre Dame Seminary.* **Below:** *Mickey Monceaux of Lake Arthur uses his boat and one in tow to bring flood victims to safety.* **Facing page:** *Sara Roberts of Lake Charles heads for dry land with two evacuees.*

Heroic people from all walks of life stepped up to help traumatized New Orleans citizens in their time of need following Hurricane Katrina. **Counterclockwise, starting with photo above:** *Doug Bienvenu and Drue LeBlanc, a Breaux Bridge couple, rescued hundreds trapped in their homes by the floodwaters. Dr. Victor Tedesco IV directed the evacuation of Touro Infirmary. Nurse Holly Broussard worked seven 12-hour shifts in a row to care for helpless patients at West Jefferson Medical Center. State Rep. Don Cravins Jr. of Opelousas helped guard prisoner-evacuees and comforted citizens in distress.*

– Photo by Freddie Herpin, *The Opelousas Daily World*

America's Hurricane Darlings: Tanisha and 'Mama Nita'

After an ordeal that could have cost them their lives,
these two neighbors and the girl's grandma are
safe and sound in Houston.

By Michael Graczyk
The Associated Press

When the TV is off and the only sounds in the neat, three-bedroom house come from the hum of the air conditioner and the gurgle of an aquarium, 89-year-old Nita LaGarde sometimes has to fight back tears as she falls asleep in her white wooden bed with clean linens.

"This is nice," she says.

The tears are not so much for what she lost, but for what she has found – a new life and new, loving friends in Houston, a city she had never even visited until September 2005 during the culmination of a hellish journey.

America met Mama Nita, as she is known, and 5-year-old Tanisha Belvin as they fled the horror of the New Orleans Convention Center in the days immediately following Hurricane Katrina.

A grim-looking Ms. LaGarde was seen sitting in a wheelchair, her withered white hand clasping Tanisha's tiny black hand, in a Sept. 3 photograph taken by Eric Gay of the Associated Press. The photo of their rescue from the convention center was published on front pages around the nation, and the pair became a symbol of the disaster.

"I wasn't going to let her go," Ms. LaGarde says of her tight hold on Tanisha in the photo.

Also with them, but out of the picture, was Earnestine Dangerfield, 60, Tanisha's grandmother and Ms. LaGarde's neighbor of 20 years at the duplex they shared in New Orleans' flooded Ninth Ward. Now, all three are living under the same roof in Houston, courtesy of a local couple.

The three escaped the rising waters in New Orleans by climbing into the attic, then punched a hole in the roof. With Ms. LaGarde and Tanisha tied to Ms. Dangerfield with an orange electrical cord, the three were rescued by neighbors in a canoe. They were taken to a bridge, where they stayed for two days.

From there, a helicopter took them to a freeway overpass, then a police truck moved them to a spot outside the Convention Center, where they waited amid the squalor for more days – Mama Nita trading a spot on the concrete for a mattress from a looted hotel. Finally, with fears for Ms. LaGarde's declining health, soldiers summoned a helicopter to pluck them from among the thousands waiting to get away.

"They kept us together," Ms. Dangerfield says. "I told them: 'Where she goes, I got to go.'"

All they had were the clothes they were wearing and Ms. LaGarde's mattress as they boarded a plane for Houston, 350 miles away.

"We've been through hell," Ms. LaGarde says. "I didn't worry. I just wanted to be out of there."

They received medical treatment in Houston, then a spot at the city's Reliant Center shelter. They were moved again, to an adjacent arena, and then once more to a motel in the suburb of Tomball.

That was where they were when the *Houston Chronicle* followed up on the AP's Page 1 photo, which had prompted many calls from readers wishing to help. The story moved a retired

Houston couple, Joe and Daisy Maura, to offer them a vacant rent house.

"We got our kids together and told them what we were going to do," says Daisy Maura, 67, who retired in August after 45 years as a Houston public school teacher and principal. "We're going to adopt this family."

"You know good people when you see them," says her husband, 68, a retired school basketball coach. "You think: They're just family. Now they're part of us. They are not here alone."

The Mauras got in touch with emergency officials, who put them in contact with Ms. LaGarde and Ms. Dangerfield.

"This is too good to be true," says Ms. Dangerfield, a former bus driver in New Orleans. "When I walked in the door, I dropped to my knees. This is better than I had in New Orleans."

"I feel like a millionaire," Ms. LaGarde adds.

Ms. LaGarde was born in Smoke Bend, La., and moved with her family in 1937 to New Orleans, where she worked in a plant that made airplane parts, as a waitress and for 10 years in a bakery at night while raising a son and daughter. Her husband died in 1986.

"I ain't going back no more," she says. "There ain't nothing to go back to."

During the interview, Tanisha was in perpetual motion, tugging at her grandmother, then racing around the living room. She was shy with strangers but cuddled up to Daisy Maura as if the woman were a lifelong relative. In her room, the little girl had her own TV, a few toys, and a choice of top or bottom bunk.

Evacuees glad to leave Superdome

After a day in line in the heat without water or food,
dozens of people passed out while waiting for a bus
to take them somewhere, anywhere.

By Mary Foster
The Associated Press

At the front of the line, the weary refugees waded through ankle-deep water, grabbed a bottle of water from State Troopers, and happily hopped on buses that would deliver them from the horrendous conditions of the Superdome.

At the back end of the line, people jammed against police barricades in the rain. Refugees passed out and had to be lifted hand-over-hand overhead to medics. Pets were not allowed on the bus, and when a police officer confiscated a little boy's dog, the child cried until he vomited.

"Snowball! Snowball!" the boy cried.

The scene played out Thursday Sept. 1 as the plodding procession out of the Superdome entered its second day – an evacuation that became more complicated as thousands more storm victims showed up at the arena.

Capt. John Pollard of the Texas Air Force National Guard said 20,000 people were in the dome when the evacuation efforts began. By Thursday afternoon, the number had swelled to about 30,000. Pollard said people poured into the Superdome because they believed it was the best place to get a ride out of town.

"I would rather have been in jail," Janice Jones said. "I've been in there seven days, and I haven't had a bath. They treated us like animals. Everybody is scared."

In Houston, after accepting more than 11,000 Hurricane Katrina refugees, officials said the Astrodome was full and began sending buses to other shelters in the Houston area Thursday night.

"We've actually reached capacity for the safety and comfort of the people inside there," American Red Cross spokeswoman Dana Allen said.

Buses that continued to arrive were being sent on to other shelters in the area and as far away as Huntsville, about an hour north of Houston.

The total of 11,375 inside the Astrodome was less than half the estimated 23,000 people who were expected to arrive by bus from New Orleans.

Pleading for patience, officials in Houston conceded they had not fully prepared for a disaster of this scale and potential duration and that they were improvising.

"Nobody came up with a plan for having this many refugees in our county," said Bill White, the mayor of Houston.

In New Orleans, an angry Terry Ebbert, head of the city's emergency operations, watched the slow exodus from the Superdome on Thursday morning and said the Federal Emergency Management Agency (FEMA) response was inadequate. The chaos at the nearby New Orleans Convention Center was considerably worse than at the Superdome, with an angry mob growing increasingly violent.

"This is a national disgrace. FEMA has been here three days, yet there is no command and control," Ebbert said. "We can send massive amounts of aid to tsunami victims, but we can't bail out the city of New Orleans."

After a day in line in the heat without water or food, dozens of people fell out. Medics poured water on them, fanned them, and tried to cool them down.

One woman, lying on a canvas cot, was in convulsions.

Medics doused her with water and slapped her, trying to bring her around. A National Guardsman poured water on a baby he held while water was also poured on her mother.

By early afternoon, a line of people a half-mile long snaked from the Superdome through the nearby Hyatt Regency Hotel, then to where buses waited. State Troopers, making every effort to be cheerful, handed out bottles of water and tried to keep families and groups together.

The situation in the back of the line was vastly different.

National Guard members stood side by side with rifles. Luggage, bags of clothes, pillows and blankets were strewn in the puddles.

After a teenager was taken away by police for fighting, a Texas Air Force National Guard official told the crowd on public address:

"We can't have people fighting. I have kids here who are crying and frightened and can't find their parents. Be adults. We're going to get you out of here. It takes a while. I'm not God. If I was, you'd all be home with your family."

Acadian Ambulance and Air Med played huge roles in hurricane rescues and evacuations

The Lafayette-based company coordinated the evacuation of thousands of people in need of medical attention, moving them out of New Orleans, Lake Charles and other cities in helicopters and ambulances.

By Don Allen

As bad as it was, the death and destruction caused by Hurricane Katrina could have been much worse. That many more lives were not lost is due in large part to the efforts of Acadian Ambulance Service of Lafayette.

By the time Katrina made landfall, on Monday August 29, most New Orleanians with the means to leave the city for higher ground had done so. But tens of thousands of other residents – including many in need of medical care – remained. Many of those who were confined to beds, either in their own residences or in nursing homes, had already been evacuated by Acadian Ambulance.

"We handled 700 evacuations in less than 36 hours before Katrina even made landfall," says Acadian Ambulance CEO and chairman Richard Zuschlag.

Acadian Ambulance had put its "Hurricane Plan" into effect several days earlier, when company executives met with the directors of the various departments, including field operations, communications, fleet maintenance and medical supply. Under normal circumstances, Acadian Ambulance has a daily contingent of 160 ambulances on duty, but for Katrina they added another 50 ambulances and called in every off-duty medic who was able to work. The seven Air Med helicopters always in commission were increased to 10, a number that soon doubled with the addition of more helicopters from other companies. After the hurricane, more than 100 aircraft were used in evacuation and rescue efforts. Even Acadian Ambulance office workers and paramedic instructors, most of whom are medics, were pulled from their regular duties to help in the emergency.

"We were working 12-hour shifts, seven days a week for two and a half weeks," says Mike Burney, operations manager in Acadian's communication center. "Employees normally behind a desk were in the field, and they did an outstanding job."

Within four days of the hurricane's landfall, Acadian Ambulance had coordinated air and ground medical evacuations from seven New Orleans hospitals – a total of 5,000 patients and people in need of medical assistance as well as hospital staff and family members. Designated as coordinator of all air medical evacuations by the State Office of Emergency Preparedness, Acadian Ambulance and Air Med evacuated some 2,000 patients by themselves, according to company officials.

In addition to those evacuated from hospitals by helicopter, Acadian Ambulance transported hundreds of sick or injured people in ambulances from staging areas on Causeway Boulevard and other dry spots in the city. Mostly, these patients were people who were rescued from their flooded homes. They got to the staging areas by boat, by airboat, by Coast Guard or Army helicopter, or on foot, having waded through the floodwaters.

"The State knew we had medically configured aircraft already in place, and that's why they called on us," Burney says.

Within days of Katrina's landfall, Acadian Ambulance became the communication center for coordinating the efforts of all civilian aircraft involved in the evacuation and rescue efforts.

The military coordinated their own medical evacuation efforts and soon asked Acadian Ambulance personnel to join them in their command post to further facilitate the movement of private air medical traffic.

But no amount of planning prepared evacuation officials for the chaos at the Louisiana Superdome, where some 25,000 evacuees were housed. While told to bring provisions for three days, many of the evacuees apparently expected the dome to provide the necessities. When that didn't happen, mainly because of the flooding that paralyzed most of the city, conditions at the dome soon turned critical.

"New Orleans reminded me of pictures that I've seen of devastation in third-world countries," says Ray Bias, Acadian's government relations manager.

A former Marine medic in Vietnam and an Acadian Ambulance employee for more than 30 years, Bias stayed at the dome for a stretch of 72 consecutive hours before taking a break.

"There were people crowded upon each other, a lack of plumbing and electricity, human and animal waste everywhere, and people with nothing more than what they had on their backs," Bias reports.

On the day after the storm made landfall Bias was joined by 10 more Acadian Ambulance paramedics and four physicians, all of whom manned the aid station at the dome.

Bias saw most of the chaos first-hand. When he returned to New Orleans after a day's rest, he found thousands of refugees still housed at the dome living under rapidly deteriorating conditions.

"It was just deplorable," he says. "Most of them were outside because they couldn't stand the stench inside.... I've seen a lot and I've been through a lot, but I was really affected by this happening inside the United States, especially because it lasted so long and without someone coming to the rescue. There weren't enough helicopters and there wasn't anybody to say,

'Look, here are your assets, I'm sending them to you, let's get the job done.' There may have been chiefs out there, but they weren't communicating with each other."

Bias says he was able to communicate only with his headquarters, through a satellite phone, but with no one else. The storm had completely knocked out the usually reliable forms of communication, even those used by the ambulance service.

"There seemed to be a lot of confusion when I went to the communications center (in New Orleans) to try and talk with the folks in charge, and even satellite phones weren't dependable all the time. Sometimes it seemed I had to go outside and stand on one leg and point to the east to even get a signal," Bias reports.

State and city officials have received criticism from the media and others for their apparent failure to communicate properly during the crisis, but Bias notes that the disaster was of such a magnitude that communication was almost impossible at times.

"We had to relay information from one entity to another for the powers-that-be to get things rolling," he says. "That hurt us because we couldn't get the sick people out of there fast enough."

But that wasn't for lack of trying. One Acadian Ambulance employee, Mike Sonnier, is credited with creating a needed landing zone atop the Tulane Medical Center parking garage by cutting down light poles, which enabled medical helicopters to reach patients trapped in that hospital. The facility had been turned into an island by floodwaters, and the makeshift heliport was instrumental in evacuating several thousand patients, employees and families from three separate hospitals.

Burney, who remained at the communication center in Lafayette throughout the crisis, credits the Iberia Parish Sheriff's Department with invaluable assistance when they volunteered the department's communication trailer to help ease the communication difficulties. With the power gone in New Orleans, the towers were inoperable, while land lines and cell phones were inconsistent at best.

The entire rescue and evacuation process was hampered by communications problems, Zuschlag points out.

"We were (eventually) asked by the military to set up our communications personnel in conjunction with theirs at the Superdome and at the Belle Chasse Naval communications center," he notes.

Before Katrina, Acadian ran approximately 160 ambulances in their 34-parish service area. Since the storm, 28 more ambulances have been added, many of which were needed in late September when Hurricane Rita moved ashore south of Lake Charles.

"For Rita," says Bias, "we had basically the same responsibilities as we did for Katrina in trying to evacuate a lot of the nursing homes and making sure people got to higher ground. Rita went a lot smoother because we already had hundreds of medical personnel from other ambulance companies. Katrina gave us a baptism by fire, but a lot of things were already in place when Rita hit."

Two weeks after Rita hit, the ambulance service was continuing to return evacuated patients to their nursing homes in and around Lake Charles, as well as in the New Orleans area. It would be a while before life at Acadian Ambulance would be back to normal.

Why the levees failed...

The breaching of the levees caused the flooding of New Orleans as Lake Pontchartrain poured into the city. But could any levee system have withstood the awesome power of Hurricane Katrina?

By Patricia Gannon

No doubt, Hurricane Katrina and the flooding of New Orleans will be the stuff of song and legend for years to come.

There will be many stories told about the day the hurricane whipped the Gulf of Mexico into a 12-foot storm surge and drove it toward the levees of New Orleans.

The storm sent millions of gallons of Lake Pontchartrain over the 25-year-old levee at 17th Street and various flood walls, putting the city underwater just hours after residents thought they had escaped the worst. Counterclockwise winds shoved part of the lake over the 8-foot seawall at Lakefront Airport. Additional breaks in Gentilly and St. Bernard Parish allowed 800,000 acre-feet of water to reach the suburbs, while levees on the west side of the 17th Street Canal held, or seemed to hold.

So, why did the levee system fail?

Simply put, the levees failed because they weren't designed for a hurricane as strong as Katrina, but were designed to withstand the surge produced by a Category 3 storm, or a weaker one, according to Al Naomi, project manager for the East Bank Lake Pontchartrain Hurricane Levee System.

Dr. Paul Richards, professor of civil engineering at the University of Louisiana at Lafayette, offers a more involved explanation for the flood.

"Yes, the hurricane came through and created the storm

surge," Richards says. "But there are any number of failure modes that could have happened."

One possible explanation for the breaches is "overtopping" of the levees. Designed for a lesser hurricane, a more powerful storm would move so much water that it would flow over the tops of the levees.

"Just think about water flowing over a levee," says Richards, who teaches levee construction, environmental engineering and waste water management. "It erodes a channel that grows deeper and wider as soil is carried away down the dry side. The more this happens, the wider it gets."

The initial storm surge that poured over the concrete wall of the 17th Street Canal dug a 26-foot-deep gouge on the other side, resulting in the failure of several wall panels and flooding much of the city, according to the U.S. Army Corps of Engineers. Photographs indicate the same thing may have occurred along London Street Canal in Gentilly and segments of the Inner Harbor Navigation Canal that gave way and flooded Chalmette.

Another possible failure mode is called "piping," Richards explains. This occurs when water pressure builds up on the wet side of the levee and causes minor flow underneath. As water pressure builds, the flow increases.

"When the river got up high years ago at Angola Prison, inmates and the Corps of Engineers sandbagged the 'springs,' Richards says. "The little flowing springs created from piping carry soil, and the more soil carried through, the more the levee is undermined."

The third possibility is that the force of the water behind the levee is simply strong enough to push the levee down, to push it back, to break it.

A fourth possibility for failure of the levees is a combination of the other three: overtopping, piping, and the levee being overpowered by the pressure of the water.

* * * * *

Shelly Moczygemba, a civil engineer who worked for the Corps of Engineers for three years on hurricane-protection projects along the Mississippi River and in the Atchafalaya River Basin, was involved with the "Unwatering Plan" for the New Orleans area.

"Nobody could predict exactly what would occur with a large hurricane, but it is the Corps' job to build and maintain the system. I remember sitting down with a topography map of the ground elevations of floodgates and seawalls. It was overwhelming," she says. "I never thought I'd see this plan go into effect during my lifetime."

New Orleans is a bowl-shaped city situated as much as 10 feet below sea level in some places. It is dependent upon a network of levees, canals and pumps to prevent flooding from Lake Pontchartrain on one side and the Mississippi River on the other. The focus of the Unwatering Plan is how to get the water out of the city if the city were to flood. She explains:

"Relying on the pumps alone doesn't get it out fast enough. In order to speed up the process, you must breach the levees and let gravitational drainage drain the city. I worked on a team, and my responsibility was to identify the best places to breach the levees....

"The reality is that a huge force of nature overpowered New Orleans. No level of engineering, experience, money and preparation can guarantee protection from a disaster."

Moczygemba is correct. There is currently no defense against a surge from a major storm. Such storms can bring surges of 20 to 30 feet above sea level, enough to top any levee in south Louisiana.

Richards agrees:

"It takes a tremendous amount of money to build levees to withstand a Category 5, and we had a Category 5. End of discussion."

According to NASA, Katrina was a Category 5 as she barreled down on Buras, but was downgraded to a strong Category 4 just prior to landfall.

*   *   *   *   *

For many, the problem with Hurricane Katrina was not a lack of anticipation, but a lack of preparation. Several state and national media organizations have observed that diverting the flow of Federal dollars from the Southeast Louisiana Urban Flood-Control Project eroded more than just levees. Spending pressures due to the war in Iraq and homeland security programs, coupled with Federal tax cuts, all but drained the flood-control project. At least nine articles in *The Times Picayune* from 2004 and 2005 specifically cite these as the reasons hurricane and flood-control dollars dried up. The same articles also predicted serious consequences.

New Orleans *CityBusiness* published an article on February 16, 2004, echoing the same viewpoint and reporting that President Bush proposed spending less than 20 percent of what the Corps of Engineers said was needed to shore up Lake Pontchartrain. *The Times Picayune* also noted that Al Naomi, the project manager for the East Bank Lake Pontchartrain Hurricane Levee System, went before the East Jefferson Levee Authority "begging for $2 million for urgent work Washington was now unable to pay for." He cited staying ahead of a potential disaster as a key to protecting the city.

"The system is in great shape," Naomi was quoted as saying. "But the levees are sinking. Everything is sinking and we need the money... to raise them."

Despite the worst hurricane season in decades in 2004, the Federal government came back in the spring with the deepest reduction of hurricane and flood funding in New Orleans history. The Corps of Engineers' office had to impose a hiring freeze; nor was the money there to fund previously proposed research to determine what New Orleans must do to protect against a Category 4 or Category 5 storm. The $10.4 million – down from $36.5 million – was too scant to begin any new projects.

One project a contractor had been racing to finish by the summer of 2005 was a bridge and levee job at the 17th Street Canal, the site of a major breach from Katrina. Similar pleas for Federal funding to offset erosion and restore Louisiana's coastal areas – the state's first line of defense against hurricanes – have met similar fates.

As coastal islands and marshes fragment, they are unable to buffer storm surges. As a result, hurricanes retain their strength longer, making it possible for them to deliver their destruction farther inland. Paired with long-term subsidence (the gradual sinking of delta areas) and a slowly rising sea level, New Orleans found itself three feet lower than it was a century ago. This combination proved to be deadly.

New Orleans has always been vulnerable to a catastrophic flood. It is in a geographically challenged place – an open invitation to a nearly perfect storm to create the worst natural disaster in U.S. history. It was only a matter of time.

Devastating hurricanes leave many with long-term stress disorders

Like combat veterans, many people directly affected
by Hurricanes Katrina and Rita are burdened
by Post-Traumatic Stress Disorder.

By Patricia Gannon

While pumping the water from New Orleans city streets was a daunting task, washing away the mental images from the minds of those who survived Hurricane Katrina may be more so.

Dr. David Dawes, a board-certified psychiatrist with Lafayette's Neuropsychiatric Clinic, says mental health agencies have observed a significant increase in individuals with Post-Traumatic Stress Disorder (PTSD), a condition that frequently develops in those exposed to catastrophic situations.

A common affliction of the military, PTSD is a medical diagnosis defining symptoms that persist longer than a month in anyone who's suffered a life-threatening event. While as many as 30 percent of the armed forces who have been in a war zone could develop the disorder, the incidence among the civilian population is normally only three and a half percent. Dr. Dawes has seen these numbers change.

"Hurricane evacuees not only had the storm trauma to contend with – knowing it's coming, evacuating and seeing the roof ripped off – but many witnessed subsequent shootings and rapes. Add to that the fact that some were traumatized before the disaster, making them even more vulnerable," he observes.

Dr. Dawes says there are distinct components to the disorder.

First is witnessing the event itself – death, serious injury, natural disaster, war or violent crimes, such as mugging or rape. Second, there's the response to the threat – fear, horror or helplessness recreated and re-experienced as flashbacks, nightmares or intrusive thoughts. Third is a biological reaction when the person shows a fight-or-flight response, shaking, anxiety or even panic.

"The fear can be paralyzing, like a deer in the headlights, or cause the individual to run away or fight," he says. "This reaction's not appropriate at work or in everyday life."

Psychiatrists recognize two types of the disorder, each characterized by its duration. Acute Stress Disorder lasts a minimum of two days and maximum of four weeks and occurs within four weeks of the traumatic event. It lasts a short period of time and fully resolves. Post-Traumatic Stress Disorder lasts at least a month, is considered chronic after three months or more, and can be delayed in its onset following the event. In addition to the distinct components, victims can also seem dazed, detached, disbelieving or stuck in the trauma and can exhibit hyper-vigilance and irritability and be prone to outbursts of anger.

Not everyone involved with Katrina did or will develop the disorder, and predicting who will or who won't is difficult.

"You can have a big, tough guy who might, and a 90-year-old lady who'll shrug and say, 'I've seen worse,'" Dr. Dawes says.

PTSD can be complicated by the fact it occurs frequently in conjunction with related disorders like depression, substance abuse, or memory problems. It can also lead to job woes and marital problems or divorce.

Whatever the degree or diagnosis, there are many treatments available, says Dr. Dawes. He advises proper screening, not once but over time, for anyone suspected of developing PTSD. Cognitive behavioral therapy explores the meaning the victim has attached to the event and attempts to reframe it in a different perspective. It is done under the guidance of a mental health professional, as is hypnosis, another treatment sometimes used to detach the bodily response from the memory.

There is also Eye Movement Desensitization and Reprocessing (EMDR), a complex process that combines the two previously noted techniques. The goal of treatment is to make the stimulus (what triggers the episodes) less arousing.

"That part of your brain that's hardwired for your survival is very powerful," Dr. Dawes explains. "It's not a simple matter of talking yourself out of it."

A group of drugs known as SSRIs (Selective Serotonin Reuptake Inhibitors) such as Zoloft and Paxil are often helpful, but simple measures are also beneficial, including avoidance of televised replays of hurricane footage, alcohol and drugs. Instead, Dr. Dawes recommends routine sleep, healthy diversions with friends, and turning to some type of belief system for support. While he says it's in the best interest of those with PTSD symptoms to seek treatment, even simple human connection can provide some psychological first aid.

The psychiatrist cites a study that shows evidence that child victims of hurricanes who were allowed to talk about the events within a few days fared better than those who weren't.

An Airboat on the Streets of New Orleans

A Cajun couple lends a hand after Hurricane Katrina floods the city

(An excerpt from the book by the same name)

By Trent Angers

Douglas Bienvenu squirmed nervously in his easy chair as he watched TV coverage of the approaching hurricane. The storm was awesome, massive, covering two-thirds of the Gulf of Mexico. It was creeping ominously toward the Gulf Coast and was a day and a half away from making landfall.

Doug knew if the hurricane were to hit New Orleans, or anywhere near, that the levees and seawalls protecting the city would give way and that the ensuing flood would be catastrophic. About half of the city is below sea level, eight feet or more in some areas, and thus is especially vulnerable to any above-average tidal surge.

The evening wore on, and it seemed inevitable to Doug that Hurricane Katrina, packing winds of 145 m.p.h., would hit New Orleans, or come very close. So he got on the phone.

"This is Doug Bienvenu in Breaux Bridge, Louisiana. I'm calling to tell you that when the levees break I can get 40 guys with airboats into the city within three hours," he told the man who answered the phone at Coast Guard Command Center in New Orleans.

"We appreciate that, Mr. Bienvenu. We'll get back to you."

Doug was fairly sure that the guy he was talking with was not taking him seriously, so he kept him on the phone.

"Now, listen, I'm telling you that storm is going to break those levees, and you guys are going to need all the help you can get," Doug said with certainty in his voice.

"And you know this because of what?"

"I've been cleaning up after hurricanes for a lot of years, and I know the power of these things..."

"Well, listen, Mr. Bienvenu, all I can tell you right now is that I'll hang on to your number, okay?"

"Listen, I'm telling you, New Orleans is going under."

The conversation ended, and Doug was red in the face. He was frustrated, angry and a little humiliated that the Coast Guard dispatcher seemed to think he was some kind of a nut.

Doug's fiancée, Drue LeBlanc, was sitting next to him on the sofa and listening as he talked to the Coast Guard office.

"Sounds like he doesn't believe you," she said.

"Hell, no, he doesn't believe me. But he's going to change his tune when those levees break," Doug fumed.

"Did you call the State Police yet?"

"Yeah, I already called them – and the New Orleans police, the Corps of Engineers, and the Wildlife and Fisheries people."

"And what did they say?" Drue asked.

"Nothing... zip... not a thing. All they did was take my name and number. They didn't seem too worried either."

Doug started pacing and mumbling, into the kitchen, then back to the den, into the kitchen, back and forth, back and forth.

The TV in the den was tuned to CNN, and the hurricane was being discussed, though it was too soon for the weathercasters to pinpoint where it would come ashore.

Doug went outdoors to get some air and began fidgeting with something in his airboat. The sky was filled with dark, heavy clouds that seemed closer to the earth than normal. He paced up and down the driveway of his modest wood frame house.

Four or five miles to the east is the Atchafalaya River Basin, where he did a lot of hunting and fishing in his younger days and where he had some of his earliest experiences driving an airboat. A few miles to the north is Interstate 10, a heavily traveled speedway that runs through a cluster of casinos, gas stations/convenience stores, fast food restaurants and Cajun cafes that serve crawfish etouffee, boudin and other south Louisiana delicacies.

*   *   *   *   *

Doug Bienvenu is a slightly nervous, talkative fellow in his early forties who studied engineering at LSU for a few years, following in his father's footsteps. He learned early in life that he dislikes working in an office and enjoys doing physical work, which he considers good for the body and the mind. The tools of his trade are his airboat and his chain saws. At 5-foot-9 and 200 pounds, he's a strong, stocky fellow with a rugged, weather-beaten look, having spent countless hours in his airboat on the bayous and in the bays and marshes of coastal Louisiana.

He did bridge maintenance for a while and later operated a tree-cutting business for 15 years, several of which were spent doing arduous post-hurricane cleanup work. In this latter capacity he and his crew used chain saws and lifting equipment to cut and remove trees and telephone poles that crashed into houses or blocked city streets and highways in communities throughout the Gulf Coast.

Doug is not timid or retiring in any respect, nor was he shy as a boy in the 1970s when he grew up in St. Martinville in a Cajun-Catholic family of nine. He is said to have been a bit wild as a teenager and was in trouble with the law on more than one occasion later in life. He spent numerous nights in the St. Martin Parish jail for drunkenness, disorderly conduct and fighting in bars. He also spent two years in prison on a weapons charge that involved a standoff with police. He was thought of by some in his community as *pas bon* – a Cajun-French term for no good, good for nothing, beyond redemption.

Drue LeBlanc, Doug's companion of seven years, is an attractive though frail-looking woman in her late forties who has been fighting kidney disease for most of her adult life. She grew up in Parks, a village between Breaux Bridge and St. Martinville. She graduated from Breaux Bridge High School and was later trained as a dental assistant, a field in which she worked for a number of years. She also worked with Doug as a bookkeeper and payroll clerk in his post-hurricane cleanup business. Her family was not at all happy that she had taken up with Doug Bienvenu, the bad boy of St. Martinville.

* * * * *

Two days after Doug started calling the Coast Guard and other agencies, the terrible storm came roaring ashore over the southeastern tip of Louisiana, swamping that area under a 28-foot tidal surge, then continuing in a northeasterly direction to maul thousands of homes and businesses on the Mississippi Gulf Coast. It drowned people and their pets, brought down trees and power lines, tossed boats around like bathtub toys, and moved houses off their foundations and floated them away. The powerful winds tore apart many, many homes, and the tidal surge, when it receded, sucked some of these mangled homes out to sea, never to be seen again.

But the highest winds missed New Orleans, and so the city seemed to have been spared. Network newscasters began reporting that New Orleans had escaped with relatively light wind damage.

Then came a report that one of the levees protecting New Orleans had been breached and that there was some flooding in the lower Ninth Ward.

This report was followed by news of another breach, then

another, then another.

The tidal surge had pushed a tremendous amount of water into Lake Pontchartrain, which, in turn, put an unbearable amount of pressure on the levees and seawalls that protect the city. The levee system had met its match and was overcome by the superior force of nature. New Orleans had run out of luck.

Floodwaters poured in not from one breach but from four, seven, fifteen and more breaks in the system. For the thousands who had not evacuated – due to infirmity, lack of transportation, lack of money for fuel and shelter, or plain hardheadedness – worry turned to fear, and fear would soon give way to extreme emotional distress.

The moment CNN reported the levees were failing, Doug bounded out of his easy chair and announced he was going to New Orleans.

"That's it, I'm out of here," he shouted.

"What, Doug?" Drue said from the bedroom.

"The levees broke. I knew it. I gotta go."

"Hold on there, buddy. I'm going with you."

"You can't come, Drue. You're sick."

"I feel okay. I'm ready to go."

"Drue, you're sick, baby. If you go into kidney failure again and we're stuck out there and I can't get you back in time…"

"Doug, I'm going. I'll be alright."

"Drue, I can't take you. You're just going to slow me down."

With that, Drue began crying, then stormed back to the bedroom and slammed the door. She stayed in the room crying for half an hour while Doug was outside hitching up his airboat and packing his truck with an ice chest, bottles of water and ham sandwiches. He threw in two of his chain saws, an axe, some rope, two life preservers, two towels and two blankets.

Another brief, heated exchange ensued, with Drue arguing her case convincingly. Doug gave in and agreed that she could go with him to New Orleans.

It was Tuesday August 30 at 10 a.m. when Doug and Drue left their home in Breaux Bridge, with the airboat in tow, traveling the few miles to I-10, then heading east on the highway toward New Orleans. They had only a vague notion of what they might find when they got there. They felt sure they and their airboat would be a welcome sight to people who would be trapped in their homes by the floodwaters.

*   *   *   *   *

Before turning on the engine of his airboat, Doug stood in the boat surveying his surroundings. He looked down Jefferson Highway, and for as far as he could see there were stranded cars on the road and on the shoulder in what appeared to be two or three feet of water. Electrical wires sagged like worn out clotheslines across the road, and small groups of people trudged through the water carrying their belongings in white plastic bags.

Closer in he saw a small alligator of perhaps two feet in length, several rats perched on driftwood, a black cocker spaniel clinging to a white Styrofoam ice chest, a partially submerged lawn chair, and various plastic and aluminum containers. Everything was out of place.

He detected a peculiar and rather offensive odor in the air: a combination of gasoline, oil and raw sewage.

It was unusually quiet and still. The ordinary sounds of the city were drowned in the flood. He heard some chatter from one of the little groups of people wading, and in the distance, maybe a block or two away, someone was yelling in a frantic tone.

Water covered the land for as far as he could see. It looked as though Lake Pontchartrain had drained into the city.

Doug and Drue put in their earplugs, and Doug turned on the 425-horsepower engine. Even at idle speed, the huge blades of the propeller spun at 500 rpm, slicing the air and creating a thunderous, deafening noise.

Doug pressed the accelerator pedal and drove slowly through the water that covered Jefferson Highway, in the general direction of downtown New Orleans. Though he was anxious to start rescuing people, he proceeded with caution for fear that some submerged object could tear a hole in the bottom of his boat.

Only half a block from the point where he launched his boat, Doug crossed the parish line, leaving Jefferson Parish and entering Orleans. The parish line is the point at which Jefferson Highway becomes S. Claiborne Avenue; it's the same road, only it changes names here.

Doug made his way down S. Claiborne, dodging sagging power lines, fallen limbs and disabled vehicles. Every few blocks he'd see small groups of people wading along the street, some pushing wheelchairs with elderly people in them, some carrying babies in their arms or young children on their backs. One man and woman were pulling a child's plastic wading pool with a child in it. Like everyone else wading along S. Claiborne, they didn't seem to know where they were going. They may have thought that by making it to a major artery like S. Claiborne they might be seen by rescuers, picked up and brought to a nice, dry shelter.

But there were no high-riding Army trucks or rescue boats to be seen, except the aluminum airboat being driven by Doug Bienvenu.

Doug and Drue gave a lift to a couple of groups of people wading along S. Claiborne, packing their boat to capacity. Then Doug headed for dry land, proceeding even more slowly and cautiously than before, trying to avoid submerged obstacles that could puncture his boat and sink it.

By day's end, the airboat had transported nearly 200 people out of the flooded area. Doug then returned to his truck, maneuvered the boat onto the trailer, secured it firmly, and drove the truck off the neutral ground onto Jefferson Highway.

Soon Doug and Drue were on Causeway Boulevard and headed toward the interstate that would take them home. When they reached the area where Causeway intersects with I-10, Doug had to slow down, for this area was now filled with emergency personnel and their vehicles – ambulances, police cars, wreckers, helicopters, Army trucks.

It was much more crowded now than it was in the morning when they were stopped for a short while by a Wildlife and Fisheries agent. This intersection had become a major staging area for the official rescue effort. In addition to the rescuers, there seemed to be dozens if not hundreds of refugees milling around, waiting around, asking for food and water, hoping to get a ride, needing a place to stay.

Doug pulled up to a Louisiana State Trooper who was directing traffic.

"Hey, officer," Doug said.

"Evening, sir," the Trooper responded, observing that Doug's truck was pulling an airboat.

"What's going on?" Doug inquired.

"Everyone's getting ready to begin the big rescue effort tomorrow," the Trooper answered.

"Yeah, that's what we've been doing. We picked up a couple hundred people out of their homes, people walking in the water..."

"Who are you with?"

"Nobody. We just couldn't stand sitting around watching TV while people were drowning, so we came to help out."

"Good for you. I hope y'all are coming back," the Trooper said.

"We'll be back tomorrow morning," Doug said.

The truck moved slowly through the crowded staging area and onto I-10 westbound. They got through Metairie and Kenner and zipped over the elevated span of highway that crosses the southern shore of Lake Pontchartrain. At the LaPlace exit – where they were stopped and then waved through by the State Trooper in the morning – they saw a long line of cars stopped at the barricades, and most of them were being turned around.

Doug and Drue continued on westward, homeward, with a sense of satisfaction that they had done something really worthwhile that day. They were glad they went, despite the stresses and hassles. Both were sunburned, and Drue was weak from having not eaten all day.

With kidney disease, and having been on kidney dialysis numerous times over the previous 22 years, Drue knew all too well how fragile her health was. She knew that eating certain foods could literally poison her and make her gravely ill. So she had decided to put off eating until she would get home. By waiting, if she did get sick at least she would be home, near her doctor and near the hospital.

Her diet was so strict, in fact, that if she had deviated from it even in the least, she could have gotten sick enough that Doug would have had to abort the rescue mission and rush her back home to the hospital. She couldn't eat anything with salt, no canned meat or processed foods of any kind, nor certain proteins, nor dairy products. Adherence to the diet was, ultimately, a matter of life and death for her.

*   *   *   *   *

On the second day of their rescue mission, Doug and Drue left Breaux Bridge before dawn and headed back to New Orleans.

Drue turned on the radio and flipped from station to station listening for news of the disaster. One newscaster reported that the water was still pouring into the city from Lake Pontchartrain, from breaches in the levees and seawalls at the 17th Street Canal, the London Canal, the Industrial

Canal. Drue got the idea that the whole city was under water. The announcer reported that helicopters were dropping huge sandbags into the breaches of the levees and seawalls in an effort to slow down the rush of water and to begin to repair the breaks. Meanwhile, the area near the intersection of I-10 and Causeway Boulevard – the rescue staging area – was becoming increasingly busy. Ambulances, helicopters and rescue boats were continuing to gather there, and a coordinated rescue effort was now apparently beginning to jell. Buses, too, were starting to line up in this area, and the number of refugees from the flood was growing.

When they arrived in New Orleans, Doug followed the same route he had taken the day before, getting off Causeway Boulevard at Jefferson Highway. He drove to the same spot where he had launched his airboat on the previous day and launched again, leaving his truck on the wet St. Augustine grass.

Throughout the day, Doug and Drue brought desperate, weary people to dry land, returning each time with 12 to 15 passengers.

On the last run of the day, at twilight, Doug and Drue were driving up and down S. Claiborne Avenue, picking up people who were wading or floating in small boats, on doors, on driftwood, anything that would float. When the airboat was nearly full, Drue spotted a man and woman half a block from the avenue, wading toward them in three to four feet of water. The man was cradling a baby; the woman was waving her arms and calling for help.

Doug steered the airboat toward the distressed couple, then circled them twice to get the boat as near to them as possible. The man handed the baby to Drue, then he gave the woman a boost into the airboat. Drue then helped the man into the boat.

"Thank you, thank you," the man said with relief in his voice.

"You're very welcome," Drue responded in a weak, though sincere voice.

Drue could see that there was something wrong with the child, who appeared to be six or seven months old. Wearing only a soiled diaper, the baby girl was barely conscious, sweating and laboring to breathe.

"How long y'all been in the water?" Drue asked in an effort to distract the mother from what was obviously bothering her.

"About an hour," the woman answered in a shaky, anxious voice.

"How far away do you live?"

"Four, five blocks," she said, pointing into the neighborhood.

"Your baby's sick?" Drue asked, getting to the point of what was on the mother's mind.

"She got asthma. She needs to go to the hospital," the mother answered with desperation in her voice.

Drue patted the baby's face and chest with a wet washcloth that she dipped in the cold water in the ice chest.

"We was waiting for someone to come get us, but nobody came. We was dying in that heat, and the baby just passed out. We gotta get her to the hospital," the mother said in an anxious tone, her emotions now starting to get away from her.

Drue teared up as she watched the face of the distraught mother, who was now crying openly as she rocked her baby. Drue's focus shifted to the helpless child; she noticed the perfect shape of the delicate little hands, the angelic face with its smooth brown skin and its tiny black eyebrows and eyelashes.

Tears rolled down Drue's cheeks as she imagined the mental anguish of the parents: trapped in the flood, watching their baby suffer, unable to do anything to relieve the suffering, afraid she would die, having no choice but to leave their house and wade out in the dirty floodwaters toward the avenue in hopes of being rescued.

As the airboat moved westward on the water that covered S. Claiborne Avenue, Drue was thinking that the parents and child were fortunate to have been rescued before dark. The situation was bad enough, a true nightmare, but it would have been worse had the family been caught in the water when nighttime came, in the dark, feeling their way, unable to see anything, not knowing where to go, not knowing what dangerous thing might be in the water.

The airboat zigzagged down S. Claiborne Avenue, dodging fallen tree limbs and small motorless boats, as it made its way back toward dry land.

After dropping off most of their passengers, Doug and Drue proceeded to seek medical attention for the baby with asthma. They returned to their truck with the baby and her parents then headed for nearby Ochsner's Hospital. It was dark when they arrived at the hospital, and Drue kissed the baby then hugged the weary, anxious mother.

The baby's parents thanked Doug and Drue over and over, then headed into the hospital, which was lighted by emergency generators. The mother cradled the child while the father carried the family's belongings in two white plastic bags.

*   *   *   *   *

The morning was sweltering, humid and somewhat overcast when Doug and Drue arrived in New Orleans and approached the evacuation staging area at I-10 and Causeway Boulevard. They were pleasantly surprised, even amazed, to see it abuzz with ambulances, police cars, Army trucks and buses loading up and driving away. Rescue helicopters were landing and off-loading their passengers in a large field just off the Interstate, then taking off and heading back toward the flooded city. It was Thursday September 1, 2005, day three of the massive search-and-rescue effort that followed Hurricane Katrina.

South of I-10, on either side of Causeway Boulevard, were throngs of people, maybe 7,000, milling around on the shoulders of the road or waiting in the large shadeless fields. They sat around in small groups, tired, anxious, worried, talking about their plight and the unknown whereabouts of loved ones. Many lay on the grass or on dirty blankets staring into space, not having the energy or the reason to do anything else for now. Some shaded themselves and their children under lean-tos made of sticks and sheets. Despair and depression were on the faces of many; anxiety, even panic were in the eyes of others. But at least they were alive, and on dry land, and they knew they would have a bus ride out of New Orleans.

Everyone had a few plastic bags containing whatever they could pull together on short notice: underwear, jeans, pills, toothbrushes, little bags of peanuts, canned meat, soft drinks, photographs, CD players.

A dozen or more buses were lined up on the northbound shoulder of Causeway Boulevard, and hundreds of people were inching their way toward the doors. Some were pushing and shoving, but most were behaving in a more civil manner. The loading of buses was being supervised by representatives of various military and law-enforcement agencies. The refugees were being hustled onto the buses nearest them, seemingly without much concern for who should be going with whom. The primary goal was to get the people out of New Orleans and move them on to someplace else, anyplace but here.

The refugees who were crowded around the buses were single-minded, focused on getting aboard no matter what. The bus was their lifeline, their means of getting to food, water, shelter; the instinct for self-preservation was being demonstrated in a clear manner. They jockeyed for position and tried to get on the same bus as their friends and family members. Many succeeded; others didn't.

In the northeast quadrant of the intersection, helicopters were landing every few minutes. Coast Guard and military choppers dropped off flood victims they had plucked from rooftops, treetops, the tops of cars and from the floodwater.

Ambulance helicopters landed with patients brought in from downtown hospitals, from the Superdome and from the Convention Center. The aircraft landed three at a time in the expansive field, while three others hovered nearby waiting their turn to land, and three more lined up behind them.

The flood victims getting off the helicopters were carried or escorted to different spots of the staging area by medics, National Guardsmen or various rescue workers, depending on whether they were in need of medical care or just a bus ride to a shelter.

Those in need of medical care were evaluated at a makeshift triage center under the Causeway Boulevard overpass, set up there to shield the medical people and the patients from sun and rain. Those in need of immediate care were treated then and there. Those needing significant though not immediate medical care were put into ambulances bound for the Pete Maravich Assembly Center in Baton Rouge, where an extensive treatment center was set up by the State – complete with physicians, imaging specialists, nurses, pharmacists and various other volunteers.

The thousands of people in the crowded staging area came not only by rescue helicopter, but on foot or on Army trucks or other vehicles. They walked in from the north, south and east, some of them from a few blocks away, others from a few miles, most of them having waded from their flooded homes to the ramps that connect to elevated spans of highway.

All in all, the staging area was a beehive of rescue activity. It was obvious to Doug and Drue that the rescue operation was now in full swing. They were impressed with all the comings and goings of helicopters, ambulances, Army trucks, police cars and buses.

"Now, that's what I'm talking about!" Doug said as he proceeded cautiously along Causeway Boulevard.

"Wow! Look at all this," Drue chimed in. "There must be

10,000 people here."

"And that's just the tip of the iceberg. I wonder how many people are still trapped in their attics," Doug added.

"I don't know, but this is a pitiful sight. Look at all these people. It looks like a refugee camp in a foreign country," Drue said, as she surveyed the field of stranded humanity.

*　*　*　*　*

Doug turned off of Airline Highway onto Palm Street, into a neighborhood that was badly flooded when the nearby 17th Street Canal seawall was breached by the hurricane's powerful surge. Palm Street, a part of the long-settled Palm-Air Subdivision, is a relatively narrow road lined with shade trees and small and modest-size wood frame houses. Doug wasn't able to drive very far down this street because it was blocked by fallen trees.

Determined that this roadblock would not keep him out of the neighborhood, he drove his airboat into the limbs and turned off his engine. He cranked up his chain saw – the same one he'd used to cut fallen trees and telephone poles after other Gulf Coast hurricanes – and began cutting a path through the limbs and branches. When he completed his task 45 minutes later, his cap and his clothes were wet with perspiration.

Doug turned on his engine and continued the search-and-rescue mission, zigzagging down Palm Street and dodging every manner of debris. He and Drue spotted stranded people on the roofs of several houses, all shouting for help and waving items of clothing in an effort to flag them down.

The routine became that Doug would drive the airboat up to the front porch and the people would wade through the house then get into the boat with their belongings. Drue would welcome them and show them where to sit in order to balance the weight in the boat.

Complications arose when most of the people being rescued

wanted to bring several bags of food, clothing, jewelry, photo albums and other valuables, plus their pets. The presence of pets and excess baggage limited the number of people who could fit in the boat. Moreover, the more the boat was weighted down the slower Doug had to go, thus the fewer runs he would be able to make in the course of a day. He didn't try very hard to place restrictions on the people on this run, but he resolved to do so on the next.

Now filled to capacity, the boat retraced its path back to Airline Highway and slowly headed for the landing. The trip was an opportunity for the flood victims to see just how widespread the flooding was; it wasn't only their immediate neighborhood that was under water, it seemed to be the whole city. The extent of the flood was practically incomprehensible; some of the adults onboard stared in disbelief at the destruction of their city.

Drue wasn't among those surveying the devastation but was bent over and looking down at the floor of the airboat. She was rocking back and forth, holding her lower back. Her kidneys were throbbing; she felt weak and vaguely nauseated. The smell of death along the highway didn't help.

Doug leaned forward to talk to her at close range.

"Drue, you alright, baby?" Doug asked.

"Yeah, I'm okay."

"You don't look okay."

"I'll be alright. Just a little kidney pain, and I feel a little nauseated."

"You got some ice?"

"Yeah, I been chewin' my ice."

"You want to wait in the truck a while?" Doug asked.

"No, Doug, I'll be fine."

"You'll feel better in the air-conditioning."

"I said, I'll be fine. I didn't come all the way out here just to wait in the truck."

"Just trying to help..."

As the airboat approached the landing, Doug could see it was more crowded than earlier in the day when they began their first run. There were more boats than before, more people, even a bus. He and Drue helped their passengers out of the boat. They also off-loaded a skinny little black and tan dog, a large number of plastic bags and a few cardboard boxes.

An official who seemed to be in charge of getting people onto the bus told the people they'd have to leave some of their belongings on the side of the road, that they would be permitted to take only one bag each. The dog, too, would have to stay. The woman holding the scrawny dog protested in a highly emotional manner, and the official told her it was the law. That ended the conversation, then the woman cried uncontrollably, hugging and kissing the dog as though it were her child. She refused to get on the bus and instead began walking down the highway with her bag of belongings in one arm and her dog in the other.

*   *   *   *   *

It was now about 10 or 10:30 a.m., and the airboat was headed back to Palm Street to resume the mission. The search had barely begun when the crew came upon a two-story house with two men on the roof. They were waving their arms and calling for help.

This was the home of Bobby and Ann Nathan. Staying with them when the hurricane struck was Ann's 92-year-old mother, Helen Alexander, and a cousin named Elaine Stephens, age 59, who was visiting from Lexington, Kentucky, and who had never been through a hurricane of any size in her life, much less anything resembling the storm of the century. Ann, a retired schoolteacher, and Bobby, a long-time employee of the City of New Orleans, had lived in the house for more than 30 years.

On the day the levees and seawalls began to fail the water rose gradually and the Nathans at first were hopeful that it would stop. But it kept coming up in their home, six inches, eight, twelve, twenty, until it was five feet deep and their furniture was floating. They feared their home might be gone for good, but at least they would still have each other. Ann cried when she realized she had lost her photos, pictures of her wedding, of her children's birthday parties, of relatives now deceased. It also upset her that she had lost her recipes, particularly those written by the hand of her mother and grandmother.

The day after the flooding began, the Nathans were joined by the neighbors from across the street. While the Nathans had a second story to which they could retreat, the folks across the street – Bruce and Carol Terrence and daughter Alana, age 16 – did not. The Terrences waited nearly until it was too late to evacuate.

But when the water reached chest-deep in their living room, they made a break for the Nathan's house and the safety of its second floor. Bruce, who couldn't swim, waded in water up to his shoulders, carrying two plastic bags filled with valuables; Carol, a weak swimmer, dog-paddled, staying very close to Bruce; and Alana, like her father, carried plastic bags over her head as she waded across the street.

Their hearts were pounding when they got to the Nathans' house, entering through the front door and wading to the stairs that took them to the second story. The Nathans welcomed them and offered them dry clothes, water and something to eat. They spent the night worrying together, all seven of them, and hoping that someone would come for them soon.

Before dark, the men made an S.O.S. sign, using a black marker on a large piece of white cloth; after dark, they shined flashlights into the sky when they heard helicopters coming near. The long night went by, but nobody came. The men were afraid no one knew they were there. The women, too, were deeply concerned, particularly Ann's cousin, who was eaten up with fear.

The next morning, Carol heard what sounded to her like a lawn mower or a motorbike in the distance. The noise kept getting louder and louder, and then the airboat appeared. Being a city-dweller, Carol had never seen an airboat. She wasn't sure what it was but she was overjoyed to see the odd-looking contraption and the three people on it.

Several in the household let out a cheer; they knew their deliverance was at hand.

"Hallelujah! Thank you, Jesus!" Ann exclaimed.

"We're not going to die here after all," Bobby said.

The shell-shocked cousin from Lexington just stared at the noisy boat.

Carol jumped around and clapped her hands, knowing that she and her family would be safe.

*   *   *   *   *

As Doug's vehicle rolled westward through the shallow, oily water that covered Jefferson Highway, he and Drue observed a stream of refugees going in the same direction, trudging through the water, carrying what remained of their belongings in plastic bags, cardboard boxes and suitcases of various sizes.

The water became shallower as the truck got closer to Causeway Boulevard, and Doug noticed that the stream of refugees had increased. Scores of people – the newly homeless – were wading in shallow water, just a foot deep now, some pushing shopping carts containing their belongings, some carrying babies or toddlers, some with children on their shoulders, all headed for higher ground, all in need of the kindness of strangers.

When they reached Causeway Boulevard, Doug and Drue saw a throng of people, possibly a thousand, under the boulevard's overpass, all of them waiting for buses to come for them, all of them seemingly too tired and weak to walk any further.

With airboat in tow, the truck moved down Causeway Boulevard toward the crowded staging area they had come through in the morning. The number of refugees had dwindled considerably, but still there were a few thousand people waiting their turn to get a ride out of the city. Doug drove cautiously through the area, as people walked nonchalantly across the road from several directions, seemingly without concern for vehicular traffic.

The truck cleared the staging area, got onto I-10 and headed west. Drue was asleep before they got out of town. Doug turned on the radio and listened to music, and he could feel his tired muscles starting to relax. His clothes were soaked with perspiration.

The traffic was very heavy heading into Baton Rouge; though it was nearly 8 p.m., it seemed like 5 o'clock rush hour traffic. News reports said Baton Rouge's population had swollen temporarily by an estimated quarter of a million people from New Orleans and the surrounding area.

Drue woke up feeling sick and weak as the truck crept through Baton Rouge.

"Where are we?" she asked.

"Baton Rouge."

"How long I been sleepin'?"

"About an hour, hour and a half."

"I'm really hungry now. Can we stop for something to eat?"

"Sure, baby, but let's get past Baton Rouge first. You believin' this traffic?"

They drove through Baton Rouge, crossed the Mississippi River bridge, and stopped for hamburgers at McDonald's in Port Allen. Drue also got a cup of ice, as was her custom.

Though they were dog-tired and their money had nearly run out, Doug and Drue were glad they had had another productive day of helping the victims of the flood. It was especially gratifying to know that the people they rescued were no longer suffering from hunger and thirst and were no longer in fear of being forgotten and left to die.

Drue was now drifting in and out of sleep and Doug was continuing to talk about the memorable events of the day as the pickup truck made its way down Interstate 10 and across the Atchafalaya River Basin.

City of New Orleans honors couple who rescued hundreds

Doug Bienvenu and Drue LeBlanc, the Breaux Bridge couple who rescued nearly 800 people in their airboat following Hurricane Katrina, have received certificates of appreciation for their heroic deeds from the City of New Orleans.

The certificates were presented in a ceremony at Hotel Monteleone in New Orleans on December 12, 2006, by Capt. Robert Williams, Operations Manager for the City's Department of Homeland Security. He made the presentation on behalf of Mayor Ray Nagin and the people of New Orleans.

Three of the people who were rescued attended the ceremony and testified to the heroism of their rescuers. Bobby and Ann Nathan and their neighbor, Carol Terrence, publicly thanked Bienvenu and LeBlanc for saving their lives.

"If it hadn't been for them, we wouldn't be here today to talk about it," Ann Nathan said. "Nobody else came for us. We had an S.O.S. sign on our roof, and waved flashlights at night, but nobody came for us. But Doug and Drue came. I look on them as angels."

Albert Charlton, a lifelong resident of New Orleans and a school teacher, served as master of ceremonies.

"Doug and Drue are two of the many, many people who gave of themselves so that their fellowmen might live," Charlton said. "Thousands of people were involved in rescuing my fellow New Orleanians, and I would like to personally thank them, one and all."

Superdome reopening a joyous occasion

New Orleans Saints' sweet victory over Atlanta Falcons
on Monday Night Football helps lift the spirits of many
in the hurricane-torn Gulf Coast.

By Nancy Armour
The Associated Press

For one day, at least, New Orleans looked much as it did before Hurricane Katrina blew in and turned life upside down for anyone who's ever called this city home.

Happy people with smiles on their faces, beads around their necks and drinks in their hands filled the city streets on the evening of Sept. 25, 2006. There was joyous bedlam inside the Superdome, where it was equal parts rout, welcome-home party and revival.

Fans were on their feet all night, waving towels and cheering every move by their beloved Saints. Chants of "Who Dat?" shook the dome, and the misery and suffering that now defines this city seemed little more than a bad memory.

For anyone who questioned why the Saints would go back to a flood-ravaged city, there was your answer Monday night, loud and clear:

New Orleans still throws the world's best party. It just needs a reason.

"We understand Hurricane Katrina went through here," Saints receiver Joe Horn said. "We understood the importance of us winning that game for them. If we would have lost, I'm sure they would still be partying, sure they'd still be happy because this organization is still in New Orleans, back

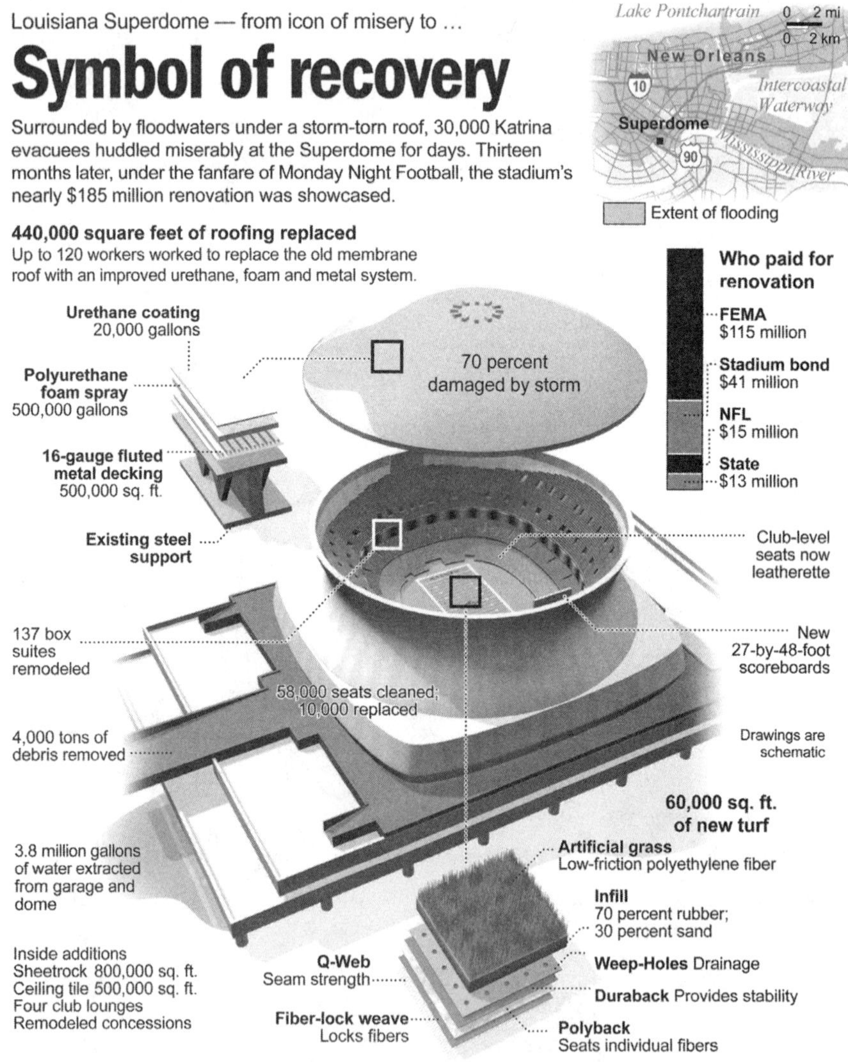
Louisiana Superdome — from icon of misery to ...

Symbol of recovery

Surrounded by floodwaters under a storm-torn roof, 30,000 Katrina evacuees huddled miserably at the Superdome for days. Thirteen months later, under the fanfare of Monday Night Football, the stadium's nearly $185 million renovation was showcased.

Lake Pontchartrain
0 2 mi
0 2 km
New Orleans
10
Intercoastal Waterway
Superdome
90
Mississippi River
Extent of flooding

440,000 square feet of roofing replaced
Up to 120 workers worked to replace the old membrane roof with an improved urethane, foam and metal system.

Urethane coating
20,000 gallons

Polyurethane foam spray
500,000 gallons

16-gauge fluted metal decking
500,000 sq. ft.

Existing steel support

70 percent damaged by storm

Who paid for renovation
FEMA
$115 million
Stadium bond
$41 million
NFL
$15 million
State
$13 million

Club-level seats now leatherette

137 box suites remodeled

New 27-by-48-foot scoreboards

58,000 seats cleaned; 10,000 replaced

4,000 tons of debris removed

Drawings are schematic

60,000 sq. ft. of new turf

3.8 million gallons of water extracted from garage and dome

Artificial grass
Low-friction polyethylene fiber

Infill
70 percent rubber; 30 percent sand

Weep-Holes Drainage

Duraback Provides stability

Inside additions
Sheetrock 800,000 sq. ft.
Ceiling tile 500,000 sq. ft.
Four club lounges
Remodeled concessions

Q-Web
Seam strength

Fiber-lock weave
Locks fibers

Polyback
Seats individual fibers

SOURCES: Ellerbe Becket; FEMA; Louisiana Superdome; Sportexe

Andy Fowle • AP

in Louisiana.

"We wanted to win to put the icing on the cake."

Too often, we make sports and the athletes who play them bigger than they are. Players refer to their games as wars. Fans who won't remember who did what to whom five years from now act as if their lives depend upon the outcome.

Sometimes, though, sport does transcend the hype and allows us to show the best of what we can be. This game – indeed, everything about this whole Saints season – was one of those rare times.

While there are parts of New Orleans that don't look any different than they did before Katrina hit on Aug. 29, 2005, make no mistake, the entire city is still struggling. The population is less than half what it was pre-Katrina, and for those who are here, every day is a fight to hang on.

Lesser cities would crumble. After decades of delighting in what sets the city apart, though, the citizens of New Orleans are finding strength in the one thing that pulls them together.

"We need this team," said Dawn Murray, dressed in Saints colors right down to her gold shoes. "It crosses all lines. It's not Democrat or Republican. It's not rich or poor. It's not black or white. It's black and gold."

And the Saints know it, giving their game ball to the city after their 23-3 rout of the Atlanta Falcons.

"This is their reward from us," Deuce McAllister said. "Three hours of joy."

It was much more than that. For one of the few times since Katrina, there was hope in the air.

Business was brisk before the game in the French Quarter, where a sidewalk saxophonist delighted tourists with a rousing rendition of "When the Saints Go Marching In" and fans waited in line for carriage tours. Aside from a few Falcons fans, the streets were a sea of black and gold. Fans in Horn, Reggie Bush, Deuce McAllister and Drew Brees jerseys. Otherwise serious-looking business men and women showing their pride in black and gold.

There was even a baby decked out in Saints paraphernalia, right down to his bib.

Around the Superdome, the transformation was nothing short of amazing.

On most days, there's little traffic in the area. Several buildings remain shuttered, the mall next to the arena is like a ghost town, and there isn't much else to entice anyone to visit.

On this day, though, it was party central. Bands played and fans milled about several hours before kickoff, happy to be killing time again before a game.

Every seat in the Superdome was filled 30 minutes before the game began, and fans danced and sang while U2 and Green Day rocked out. High up on the facade below the top deck, a simple black and white banner read, "Thank You America! New Orleans & Saints Are Here To Stay!"

"Tonight the word 'homecoming' will take on a new meaning and will forever be redefined by what is happening here in the Superdome," former NFL commissioner Paul Tagliabue said before the big game.

One game doesn't mean, of course, that all of New Orleans' problems are solved. The rebuilding will go on for years. Even the goodwill surrounding the team and owner Tom Benson will surely be tested.

There's no guarantee fans will continue to sell the Superdome out as they do year after year after year in Green Bay, New England and Indianapolis. It remains to be seen, too, if there will be the wealth to fill the luxury boxes that are the lifeblood of pro sports.

Those are problems for another day. For one night, the Saints let New Orleans forget its troubles and feel like the glorious Big Easy of old.

PART 2
HURRICANE RITA

In southern Vermilion Parish, between Erath and Pecan Island, cattle ranchers and farmers take back roads as they attempt to reach their homes after Hurricane Rita.

Photography by P. C. Piazza

Hurricane Rita's unwelcome visit to southwest Louisiana

Four weeks after Hurricane Katrina flooded New Orleans, an even more powerful storm severely damaged Cameron, Lake Charles, Sulphur and parts of east Texas.

By Jefferson Hennessy

On September 24, 2005, less than one month after Hurricane Katrina's floodwaters destroyed much of New Orleans, a second major hurricane named Rita blew ashore in southwest Louisiana, wiping out coastal homes, businesses and entire communities with storm surges of 15 feet and more. The town of Cameron was leveled except for the courthouse, the water tower and a few other structures.

Rita made landfall at 2:30 a.m. on a Saturday morning just east of Sabine Pass. While Rita raged, every parish in coastal Louisiana – from the Texas border to the mouth of the Missis-sippi River – was flooded by saltwater tidal surges.

Three days before Rita's arrival, an estimated 1.3 million people were sent packing in search of higher ground, with 250,000 evacuating areas in southeast Texas and southwest Louisiana.

Measured at Category 5, with winds reaching 175 m.p.h. and gaining strength, the storm was characterized by forecast-ers as potentially one of the most powerful ever to plow into the U.S. mainland.

Galveston, low-lying parts of Corpus Christi and Houston – plus mostly emptied out New Orleans – were under mandatory evacuation orders as Rita sideswiped the Florida Keys and began drawing energy with terrifying efficiency from the warm waters of the Gulf of Mexico. The massive storm grew in strength and size, and it appeared to be heading for Galveston.

Meanwhile, in New Orleans the Corps of Engineers raced to fortify the patched-up levees breached by surge waters from Hurricane Katrina, fearing that the additional rain and surge could cause a re-breaching of the levees and flood the vulnerable east bank area of the city all over again.

Rita roared ashore as a Category 3 storm, inundating thousands of homes with heavy rainfall and knocking out power lines with winds topping 100 m.p.h. Sugarcane, rice, and cotton fields were submerged, and fresh water marshes ended up under several feet of ruinous saltwater.

New Orleans endured new flooding as water poured into low-lying areas of the city. In communities south of the city, like the small town of Lafitte, boats were used to rescue people from homes swamped by up to six feet of water.

In Terrebonne Parish, many levees were breached, with seven to eight feet of water flooding low-lying roads.

In Vermilion Parish, boats were used to rescue people from their rooftops in tiny Pecan Island, in the marshes not far from the Gulf coast.

Some of the worst early damage was in Vinton, west of Lake Charles and near the Texas border, where several fires were burning and the roof was torn off a recreation center.

A riverboat casino and a barge in Lake Charles were knocked loose and floating free. The barge slammed into the Interstate 10 bridge spanning the Calcasieu River.

To the east of Lake Charles, in Jennings, a tornado blew away the gasoline pumps and canopy of a service station and sucked windows out of buildings. A local fire station reported its roof was rapidly peeling away.

Entergy Corp. reported nearly 300,000 homes and businesses

in Louisiana were without electricity – in addition to the more than 200,000 still lacking power from Hurricane Katrina.

The day after Rita hit, local law enforcers were greeted with a huge assist from more than 40 federal, state and municipal law-enforcement agencies.

The Maricopa County Sheriff's Office in Arizona sent 70 deputies. Ohio's Sheriffs Association sent 44 deputies, and the Tuscaloosa County, Alabama, Sheriff's Department sent 33. Eight SWAT teams worked through the night in unison with federal officers with the Marshall's Office, the ATF, the FBI and the Secret Service, bringing the total number of law-enforcement officials to more than 1,000 in Calcasieu Parish alone.

The Knox County, Tennessee, Sheriff's Department sent five helicopters to assist in search-and-rescue missions to remove stranded flood victims from inaccessible river bank communities.

After the storms, Rita and Katrina combined were estimated to have caused so much damage and financial loss that State Agriculture Commissioner Bob Odom asked the U.S. Department of Agriculture to forgive the 2005 crop loans.

The storms damaged myriad crops and commodities in all areas of the state, but the drubbing received by the rice, cotton, sugarcane and timber industries was particularly harsh. The main culprit for so much agricultural damage was saltwater.

Damage to the rice industry was estimated to be $12 million. It was $38 million for cotton, $286 million for sugarcane, and $826 million for timber.

Scores of cattle died in flooded areas along the entire Gulf coast, causing a substantial shortage in revenue for that industry.

– Additional reporting by the Associated Press

– AP Photo / *Houston Chronicle* / Brett Coomer

Traffic is lined up on the East Loop over the Houston Ship Channel as residents evacuate on Sept. 21, 2005, anticipating the arrival of Hurricane Rita in Houston.

– *Austin American-Statesman* / Matt Rourke

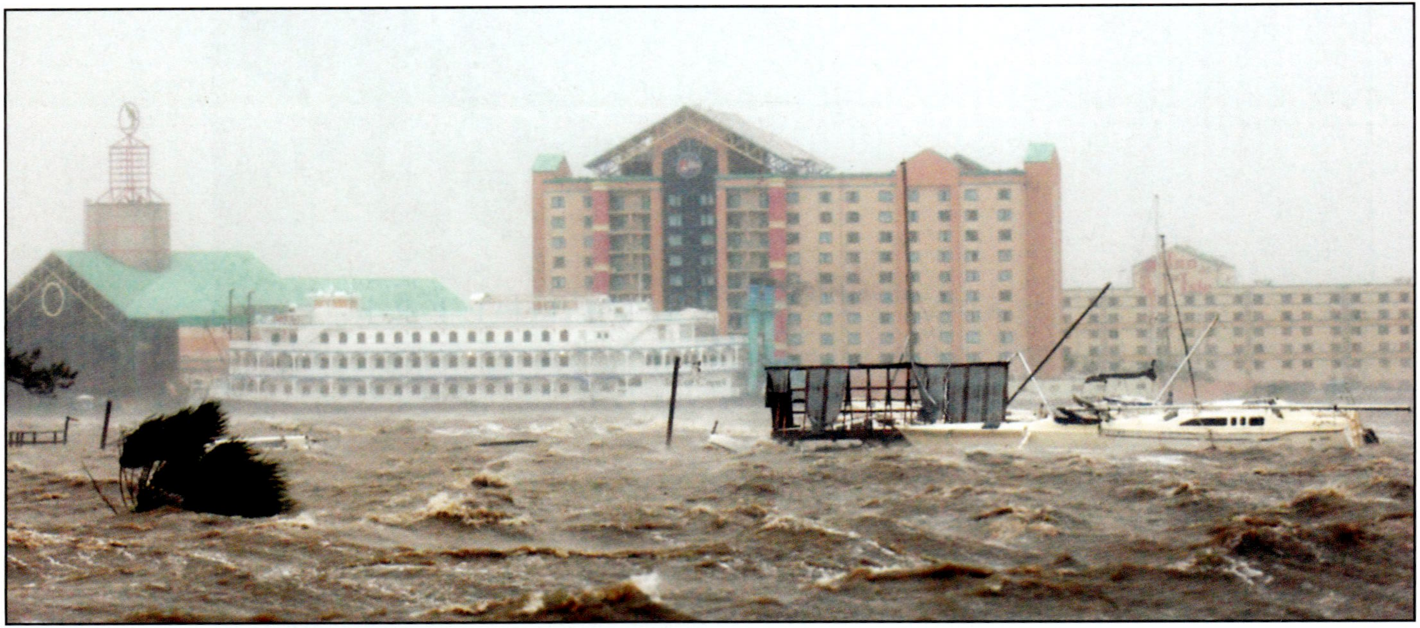

Wind-driven waves crash against boats at a marina and a casino boat near the Interstate 10 bridge in Lake Charles, La., as Hurricane Rita passes through on Sept. 24.

Members of a Marine unit based in Knoxville, Tenn., walk through floodwaters in Erath after searching a police vehicle to see if anyone was inside. The men are Cpl. Andy Gentry (foreground), Lance Cpl. David Flowers (left), Lance Cpl. Mark Gajewski, and Scott Williams. Hurricane Rita caused serious flooding in the coastal parishes of southwest Louisiana.

– Photography by P. C. Piazza

There was a house here, but only the chimney and foundation remain after Hurricane Rita barreled through southwest Louisiana.

– Photography by P. C. Piazza

Hurricane Rita completely destroyed or heavily damaged every structure in Cameron except the town's water tower and courthouse.

Hurricane Rita's storm surge caused extensive agricultural losses when it flooded much of coastal Louisiana.

Father Joseph McGrath reviews Scriptural passages to be read during a Sunday Mass at Our Lady of the Sea in Cameron 2½ years after Hurricane Rita. Like many of the town's citizens, he resumed his duties – albeit under very difficult circumstances – soon after the storm passed.

– Photography by Sherwood Cox

Cameron residents sit on the steps of a business that was washed away 2 ½ years earlier by Hurricane Rita's storm surge. Despite the extreme damage wrought by the storm, many of Cameron's residents returned home, determined not to give up on their community. Included are, left to right, Darlene Crosby, her son Paul, Belinda Miltenberger and Aaron LaSalle.

Life after Hurricane Rita

In September 2005, the coastal community of Cameron
was devastated by strong winds and a massive storm surge.
Two and a half years later, the hope, faith, frustration
and struggle of a town are evident in its citizens.

By William Kalec

Life goes on in the forgotten town of Cameron.

As the day begins, Father Joseph McGrath is preparing
Sunday's sermon for Mass at Our Lady Star of the Sea. A
man of faith, Fr. McGrath knows the message he preaches is
as important as ever, even if it reaches a congregation that is
much smaller than before Hurricane Rita.

Down the road, Belinda Miltenberger and her staff por-
tion out plate lunches inside the kitchen at GG's Cafe. It's
her mother's business, but Belinda worries about her, so she
helps out often.

Aaron LaSalle says good-bye to his wife and kids and begins
the long drive to work. LaSalle, a car salesman in Lake Charles,
won't get to the dealership for an hour. It's an expensive commute, but he just can't bring himself to uproot his family and
abandon his hometown of Cameron.

And Darlene Crosby watches as volunteer workers from a
Mennonite church in Michigan construct her new, donated
home. Without their charity, she's not sure where she'd be
living a few months from now.

All four of these folks either live or work in Cameron, and
through them the pulse of their wounded community can be
taken. The details of their personal stories are different, of
course, but the theme of recovery and rebuilding is the same.

They all hang on to hope, yet they are aware that even hope has limitations.

They find strength amongst each other because their plight seemingly has been ignored by the outside world. On September 24, 2005, Hurricane Rita made landfall at the Louisiana-Texas state line. Category 3 winds and a massive storm surge leveled Cameron, literally. Only the courthouse and the water tower were left relatively unscathed.

The national media descended upon the affected areas, searching for a sequel to Hurricane Katrina. And while they found structural devastation, the near-complete evacuation of Cameron Parish made it impossible to capture the same gripping human anguish. That's not to say it didn't exist. Two and a half years later, it still exists.

The reporters left within a week, leaving the story of Cameron largely untold.

Fr. McGrath holding up okay under a heavy burden of his own

And He who sat upon the throne said, Behold, I make all things new. – Revelations 21:5

These are a tested people.

Father Joseph McGrath knows of their frustrations, their fears, their desire to live simply, earning their way off the bountiful body of water that has erased this entire community more than once. They look to this priest for guidance, for spiritual direction, for some greater explanation to make sense of all this. He then steers them to the Scriptures, poignant passages that resonate with additional meaning, given the context of Cameron's plight.

Since Rita's landfall Fr. McGrath has blessed the mobile homes of those who've returned and blessed the uprooted caskets of those whose final resting places were disturbed by the flood.

Fr. McGrath's people are a tested people.

He knows, because he is one of them.

The bed his great-grandfather was conceived upon, the irreplaceable family heirloom Fr. McGrath slept in every night, was washed away along with other priceless items accumulated throughout the years. Like so many residents, he bought his own trailer after the FEMA trailer he was promised never arrived. Government officials called three times to schedule an inspection of Fr. McGrath's nonexistent FEMA trailer. Someday, he says, he'll own a house down here, though, like many of his people, he's not sure how or when.

Though they look to him, he hurts just the same.

That is why on this Sunday, and every Sunday at Our Lady Star of the Sea, Fr. McGrath finds time for a personal prayer before the Blessed Sacrament.

"Sometimes I'm as lost or as impatient as they are, though I try to hide it," he admits. "Sometimes, I'll just be with them and shed some tears with them. And before we're leaving, we're laughing together. I wasn't one to say 'I love you.' I would try to show my love in concrete actions, but I find since the storm that that is very important. We're all doing that, even man to man, 'I love you.'"

During Mass, a deep sense of reverence permeates the silence. Fr. McGrath delivers today's sermon – focusing on the revival of confession – to a congregation that doesn't arrive late and doesn't duck out early. Some of the women here still wear veils, and everyone who is physically able kneels for Holy Communion and receives it on the tongue.

Fr. McGrath tells his congregants to live the Gospel message heard here today, to carry it with them when they leave. But outside these church doors, residents are met with the scenery of uncertainty – empty lots where businesses used to be, temporary residences where houses used to be, portable units where the school used to be. The desolation makes Fr. McGrath's message hard to retain.

"Psalm 23, 'Even though I walk through the valley of the shadow of death,' has taken on a whole new meaning," Fr. McGrath says. "Because, at times, it's so easy to focus just on the pile of rubble across the street from where I live, just to see mountains of concrete, and there are still houses that are floating in the marsh."

A few days before the Sunday Mass, Fr. McGrath was shocked by a question asked him by a fellow priest:

"Aren't things just about back to normal down there?"

"I could've throttled him," Fr. McGrath says with a laugh.

In fact, Fr. McGrath estimates that he doesn't know the whereabouts of 30 to 40 percent of his regular pre-storm churchgoers. He's tried looking for them in updated phone books of areas like Lake Charles, Alexandria and Lafayette but suspects most of them are dependent strictly on cell phones.

When Bishop Glen John Provost of the Diocese of Lake Charles recently asked, "How are you doing, Father? Tell me truthfully." Fr. McGrath could only reply, "I'm making it up as I go along." Because of the newfound distance between Fr. McGrath and many of his parishioners who have moved to the northern half of Cameron Parish, he is unable to maintain his pre-storm schedule.

Tasks like visiting physically disabled parishioners who don't have the means to make it to church used to take up three days of a month. Now, it takes up a lot more than that.

The Rosary is great consolation to Fr. McGrath. So, too, is the passage of Matthew 6:19: "Do not store up for yourselves treasures on earth, where moth and rust destroy, and where thieves break in and steal."

Fr. McGrath is living by this Gospel admonition, as half the drawers and closets in his camper are now empty. He's downsized, he says, and that's a good thing.

"So many of Jesus' parables, He told those parables because He knew we'd remember stories, and the stories always have a point," Fr. McGrath says. "It's time for all of us along the coast to start connecting those dots. And once we grasp those points, we've got to live them."

The service has ended but many in the congregation have not left, choosing to stay for the baptism of little Sophie Ann Trahan, daughter of Jonathan and Becky Trahan. They just moved back to town and live in a converted outdoor kitchen while they wait for a more normal residence to be built.

They, too, are tested people.

A ceremony already steeped in symbolism means that much more in this church, this community. It's a sign of rebirth, a sign of recovery. The beads of water trickle down her brow, cleansing Sophie Ann of original sin as she's welcomed into a parish, into a town that God will make new.

Belinda Miltenberger's heart is still in Cameron

The phone is ringing, but Belinda Miltenberger can't find the receiver.

She follows the digital ring through a cloud of kitchen smoke that makes her clothes smell like onion rings. She brushes aside stainless steel pans, paper towels and a plastic bucket of peas before finally finding the phone.

"This is GG's," she says hurriedly. "No, I'm sorry, we're out of the plate lunch. Yep, they were gone a long time ago. Uh-huh."

Her shoulder pins the phone to her ear. Her hand is scribbling down an order for a cheeseburger, only mayonnaise and mustard. Her mind is elsewhere, occupied with thoughts of her sick father in the hospital, the logistics of getting her kids to their after school activities, and the tedious post-hurricane rebuilding process.

Her heart remains in Cameron but her faith in its full recovery is diminished. Her façade is deceiving – cheery, upbeat and genuinely inviting – because it masks the emotional turmoil shared by most everyone in this forgotten community.

"Why did we come back? This is home," she says. "This is where we're from. This is where our families are. This is where our relatives are buried. This is where my kids go to school. This is where their friends are. Even if we can't understand why this happened and why it's taking so long to rebuild, the world still makes more sense here than anywhere else for a lot of people."

At GG's, they don't count calories or worry about trans fats. Meals are served in Styrofoam containers and eaten in an outdoor dining area consisting of picnic tables covered by a carport – which harmonizes with the aura of impermanence pervading this proud and stubborn community.

Familiar faces, mostly oil rig workers, wait patiently for their food. Miltenberger yells into the kitchen (GG's intercom system, she jokes) to check on an order. Her mother opened this business in '07 despite having no previous food service experience. Workers need a place to eat, she reasoned, so why not open a restaurant? How hard could it be?

Miltenberger laughs. She's never had a tougher job.

But, for all of these restaurant employees, the frantic pace is welcome because it distracts them from the ever-present questions about the future of the business – and of the town.

Miltenberger allowed herself to cry for one day after Rita hit. After that, not a tear. That doesn't mean the pain disappeared. Rather it's been suppressed, which is in tune with the "brush it off" mentality of these people.

The women who work at GG's aren't naïve enough to think these wounds from Rita will ever heal fully. Not without time and not without help. To cope, many of the employees were prescribed anti-depressants, or "nerve pills," as they're called around here.

"I'll be honest, I stay depressed 90 percent of the time because the storm has caused me stress like you would not believe. I hate my house. I mean, I love it, but it has caused me so much stress that I wish it would burn down. I'm in this process and the process is long. Taking forever. You look for the light at the end of the tunnel and, Lord have mercy, there's no light," Miltenberger says.

"And you hear your kids, 'Mama, when are we going down to the house?' And all you can tell them is, 'I'm trying. I'm trying.'"

At around 1:15 p.m. the lunch rush has subsided. Down time at GG's is spent in the back room. Miltenberger lights a cigarette – one of those simple pleasures – and takes a puff. The crew joins her and the conversation is dominated by the subject of the long road back.

They vent about their frustrations with FEMA, insurance companies' creative assessments of damage caused by wind vs. flood, the media which have ignored their plight, and these stringent building codes. They're not looking for a handout, or a sympathetic ear, they just want to be able to rebuild without hassle, regardless of the risk.

Aaron LaSalle just can't abandon his hometown

It's 7:13 p.m., and Aaron LaSalle's busy workday is finally complete. The sun called it quits and punched out about an hour ago.

Equipped with a smooth voice and signature country charm, LaSalle sells Chevrolets and Hondas for a dealership in Lake Charles. It's not a bad job, really. He gets to interact, meet new people, and utilize his salesman's bravado to make the car's standard features sound not so standard.

On occasion, while walking the car lot, he'll run into someone from back home, someone he grew up with in Cameron. With these customers, LaSalle can be himself and just listen as they speak of the long road home and how it's filled with financial and emotional obstacles too daunting for some to overcome, leaving them unable to return.

LaSalle understands the sacrifice.

The road home for him is long, too – 52 miles long, to be exact, 104 miles round trip.

For reasons his co-workers can't comprehend, LaSalle still lives in Cameron, driving back and forth to the car dealership each day, six days a week. Asked what he spends on gas, LaSalle lets out an exasperated sigh before estimating, "about $130 a week or about $500 a month." And, of course, that figure doesn't factor in the wear and tear on the vehicle or on LaSalle's well-being.

The drive drains him. It's disturbing how well he knows this stretch of highway; he could practically drive it blindfolded. LaSalle sees the same billboards for cable TV service and fast-food joints more than he sees his friends.

On this day, the sounds of early-1990s R&B sensation Boyz II Men escort him down the road while the vibrations from the floorboard soothe his sore feet. Usually, LaSalle is so exhausted that on most nights he'll simply put on his slippers and lean back in the recliner, like an old curmudgeon, he admits. He'd probably do the same tonight except his kids want him to cook spaghetti for dinner, and he doesn't have the heart to say no to them.

After all, that's the reason LaSalle subjects himself to this grueling pilgrimage. It's for his kids.

"Say, for instance, if my kids were to grow up in Lake Charles, you'd have to keep an eye on them," LaSalle says. "You couldn't let them go to just anybody's house. You'd have to worry about all sorts of crazy stuff. Where I'm at now, my kids can go outside without being bothered. The neighbor isn't gonna do nothing crazy to them. Pretty much, it's like you're kin to everyone in Cameron.

"If I go to a bar anywhere else, they'd look at me like I was an outsider. But when anyone comes to the bar in Cameron, you're welcomed. That's how I feel down here. I'm welcome."

Before the storm, LaSalle worked in Cameron as a welder – one of many industrial jobs that has disappeared since. When LaSalle and his family returned to Cameron after evacuating to nearby Indian Bayou, the only jobs available were either on offshore oil rigs or commercial fishing boats, and, as LaSalle explains, "I'm not too good on boats."

About a year ago, LaSalle landed this job at the car dealership in Lake Charles. He and his wife weighed the pros and cons of staying in Cameron or moving north. Obviously, they'd be able to pocket much more of LaSalle's paycheck by living closer to Lake Charles. And they'd still be somewhat close to family and friends. Lake Charles is a lot more fully functional than Cameron, a lot more convenient.

Really, when he thought about it, going to Lake Charles seemed like an easy decision.

But for LaSalle, who grew up in Cameron, leaving his hometown during its darkest days would feel like abandonment. This place reared him. This place influenced him. Its temperament is ingrained in him. Asked to imagine the milestone moments in his kids' lives – graduations, weddings, birthdays, etc. – taking place somewhere else, LaSalle quickly responds, "I can't."

Comparatively, an hour commute to work is a small sacrifice for being able to remain in Cameron.

"Cameron is here, but a lot of people don't really know what Cameron was," LaSalle says. "It's not in the press. It's not in the news. Since we're not overpopulated like New Orleans, you don't hear about what's going on down here. Cameron is rebuilding itself by itself. We're not getting much help from the government and the state.

"But what good is it to complain?"

Boyz II Men plays on as the traffic subsides and the street

lights fade in the rearview mirror. LaSalle passed lower Cameron Parish's only stoplight ten minutes ago, meaning it's almost time to pull into the driveway, boil the water, and heat the spaghetti sauce for dinner.

In less than 12 hours, he'll head back up north for work, again. But for now, he's finally home.

Darlene Crosby's tale of 2 houses

The beer is cold, the mixed drinks are strong, the music is loud, and the pool tables are worn in the House that Darlene Crosby Built – or suggested be built, anyway.

"People needed a place to laugh, and The Ice House is our place," she says.

Before the storm, Crosby's friend, Ashful Authement, owned a moderately successful deli on Cameron's main drag. It wasn't overly profitable and did nothing for his soul, but it paid the bills. So after that business got wiped away, Authement simply planned to rebuild it.

That's when Darlene Crosby spoke up.

Build a bar, she suggested.

Build a place where folks can reunite every weekend, where they can vent, where barstool Hemingways can scribble limericks on the walls, where fishing nets double as window drapes.

After Crosby presented her case, Authement was convinced. He'd build and operate The Ice House – Cameron's lone watering hole. It'd be different than the deli, more fun. And, as he so eloquently stated, "My Dad drank a lot of beer, so I figured owning a bar might not be a bad business move."

The scene on this Saturday night is typical.

An oilfield worker tries to impress his friends by ordering a screwdriver with expensive vodka. The woman in the corner rolls her eyes at the inebriated coos of a gentleman caller. Jukebox continuity is non-existent as Lynyrd Skynyrd is followed by Tupac Shakur, which is then followed by Eric Clapton.

Many Ice House patrons aren't sure where they'll go in a few months, when the grace period for meeting new building codes expires. But for now, they are here, enjoying a drink.

Crosby intended to join them tonight, to catch up with friends. But instead she's asleep inside her FEMA trailer, battling the flu.

The glow from her 13-inch television illuminates her tight living quarters. Groceries are stacked atop the refrigerator because cabinet space is minimal.

"We're all living artificially" Crosby says. "I'm not living where I was before the storm. This person is not living where they were before the storm. For me, I feel artificial. This is not my land. This is not where I lived for years.

"It angers me because I have some photographs of Hurricane Audrey, 1957. One year later, you couldn't tell this town ever had a hurricane. Two and a half years later, after Rita, we have no grocery store, we have no drug store, we have no permanent schooling, and the kids are still in portables. We have a library in a double-wide. There's no sign of structure in this town, and that angers us because it gives us no closure.

"All that's still here is us."

Crosby, whose livelihood is selling shrimp caught from her brothers' commercial fishing boat, intended to put a down payment on a mobile home when she returned to Cameron. Her problem, though, was the $35,000 cost to elevate up to new building standards. She simply couldn't afford it. Frankly, she says, a lot of people in Cameron can't afford it.

And without the proper elevation, utility companies are not allowed to provide service. Some defiant residents insist they'll use generators, but, of course, that's not inexpensive, either.

More than likely, Crosby would have been left with no choice but to move out of lower Cameron Parish had Carl and Laura Dube of Fairview, Mich., not pulled into her driveway one miraculous January morning.

They got out of the truck and asked for Darlene Crosby. They were here to build her a home.

At first, Crosby thought these two strangers were pulling the cruelest of jokes. But then she noticed the Mennonite Disaster Relief logo on the door of their truck. This was real.

Then, she asked how they got her name.

"By the grace of God," they told her.

The 1,000-square-foot home is being built high off the ground (to meet elevation requirements, of course), towering above Crosby's FEMA trailer and the temporary life she can't wait to abandon. The house should be done within a month.

Inside, there will be enough pantry space for cereal boxes, enough room for her to put her things. She plans to put a pool table in the dining room. Asked where she's going to eat, she responds, "Oh, I'll just stand."

But a brief moment of laughter is quickly replaced by somber reflection.

Crosby estimates she knows at least 100 people who don't know what they'll do once FEMA takes their trailers. They'd like to remain in Cameron, but might be priced out of staying.

In this forgotten town, there just aren't enough miracles to go around.

"I feel selfish," Crosby says. "I felt greedy when they were starting to build my house, and people were turning to look and I felt not really ashamed but almost embarrassed because it was me and not Mr. and Mrs. Whoever. But, I have to say, I couldn't turn it down.

"Every night I prayed to God, asking for Him to not let these government people make me move out of Cameron when FEMA comes to take their trailers, and here was my answer (the house built by the Mennonites).

"This is closure."

PART 3

ANIMAL RESCUES

Photo courtesy of the LSU School of Veterinary Medicine

Pets rescued by the thousands by kind people from across the U.S.

It wasn't looking good for the dogs and cats trapped in flooded homes following Hurricanes Katrina and Rita. Then an army of volunteers from Louisiana and other states stepped forward to rescue the helpless animals.

By Trent Angers

While rescue workers were pulling stranded people from their flooded homes in the wakes of Hurricanes Katrina and Rita, thousands, if not tens of thousands of evacuees worried about the pets they'd left behind.

In the case of Hurricane Katrina, evacuees from New Orleans and the surrounding area had left town for major storms in years past and had left their dogs and cats at home, knowing that the animals would not be allowed in most motels nor in any shelters set up by the Red Cross.

They figured this hurricane experience would be no different, that they would return home after the danger had passed, that their pets would be safe and sound and would greet them enthusiastically upon their arrival.

That turned out not to be the case, however, as huge portions of New Orleans and surrounding area were flooded in what proved to be the worst natural disaster in U.S. history.

If the flood was a catastrophe for the people, it was a death sentence for many dogs, cats and other small animals that were trapped in their homes as the water rose around them. It must have been a terrifying experience for the helpless animals with their owners gone and no one home to save them.

Filled with anxiety over the fate of their pets, people paced nervously in their shelters and motel rooms. They began making phone calls, to the police, to the Coast Guard, to the Louisiana Society for the Prevention of Cruelty to Animals (LA/SPCA).

The LA/SPCA received thousands of calls from New Orleans area residents, asking them, begging them to rescue their animals and providing addresses where they could be found.

But, unfortunately for the animals and their owners, the first order of business in this chaotic, overwhelming disaster was the rescue of human beings.

Very few animals were rescued at the same time that people were being plucked off their roofs or helped out of their flooded homes. That's because U.S. Coast Guard helicopter teams were instructed to retrieve people only, not pets. Rescuers in boats from various agencies were given similar instructions.

Many stranded people – some of them camped out on their roofs and baking in the sun – refused to leave without their pets. Abandoning a beloved pet was unthinkable to some, simply not an option. This is the same reason why some people declined to evacuate in the first place, before the storm: They knew their pets would not be allowed in most motels or in any of the shelters set up by the Red Cross – and they were not going to be separated from their pets under any circumstances, period.

On the other hand, many thousands of people did evacuate with their animals before the storm and were able to place them in shelters in the same cities where they (the people) took refuge. For instance, animal shelters were set up at Blackham Coliseum in Lafayette, at LSU's John M. Parker Coliseum in Baton Rouge, and at various facilities in Monroe, Shreveport, Alexandria, Thibodaux and other cities.

Back in New Orleans, the LA/SPCA was initiating a major animal-rescue operation, with hundreds of volunteers from Louisiana, California, Texas, Mississippi, Florida, New York,

Vermont and other states. In addition to the LA/SPCA, numerous agencies were involved in the effort, including the American SPCA, the Humane Society of the U.S., Best Friends Animal Society, United Animal Nations, Southern Animal Foundation and International Fund for Animal Welfare.

The animal-rescue operation was based at the Lamar Dixon Center in Gonzales, off Interstate 10, between New Orleans and Baton Rouge.

The center was set up essentially as a shelter of first resort, a staging area, for both small and large animals. Veterinary services were provided by members of the Louisiana Veterinary Medicine Assn. and Veterinary Medical Assistance Teams (VMATs), who worked in cooperation with the U.S. Public Health Service. The job of setting up the center was coordinated by the Louisiana Department of Agriculture, which includes the Office of the State Veterinarian.

With some 500 small-animal rescuers on hand to help at one time or another, LA/SPCA leaders divided the New Orleans area with a grid of 39 sections and assigned teams of rescuers to each.

They went house to house, breaking and entering with crowbars and sledge hammers in their heroic efforts to find and save the helpless animals. They found many animals dead from starvation or drowning. They found others alive but weak from hunger, dehydration, stress and/or exposure to contaminated water. There were many sad and tearful experiences, and many moments of joy and triumph as the rescuers lovingly carried their fellow beings to safety.

Some 8,500 pets were saved and transported to the Lamar Dixon Center, where they were routinely fed, washed, examined, identified, labeled and listed so they could be located by their owners. Thousands were logged in on the website, petfinders.com. Pet owners were able to use the website to track and reclaim their animals. After spending some time at the Lamar

Canine refugees look around with curiosity after being rescued from the clutches of Hurricane Katrina and its floodwaters. The guys doing the dog-sitting are Henry Rivet, an EMT-paramedic with Acadian Ambulance Service (left), and Marc Creswell, a flight paramedic. The men were at the Chalmette Slip triaging medical patients and agreed to watch the puppies while their owner took a lunch break.

Rows of cages temporarily housing small animals were spread out across the floor in the Hurricane Katrina Emergency Animal Shelter at LSU's John M. Parker Coliseum in Baton Rouge in September of 2005. The shelter housed dogs, cats and assorted pigs, rabbits, guinea pigs, ferrets, hamsters, gerbils, mice, tortoises and birds.

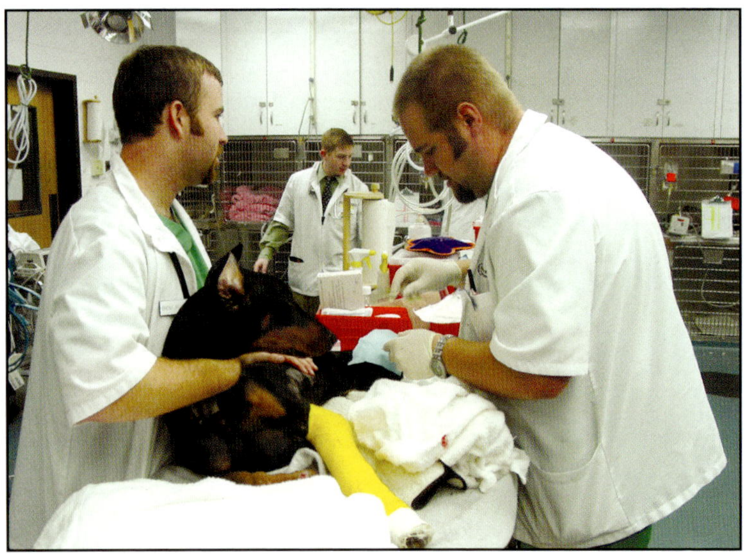

Volunteers at the John M. Parker Coliseum care for a dog with a broken leg.

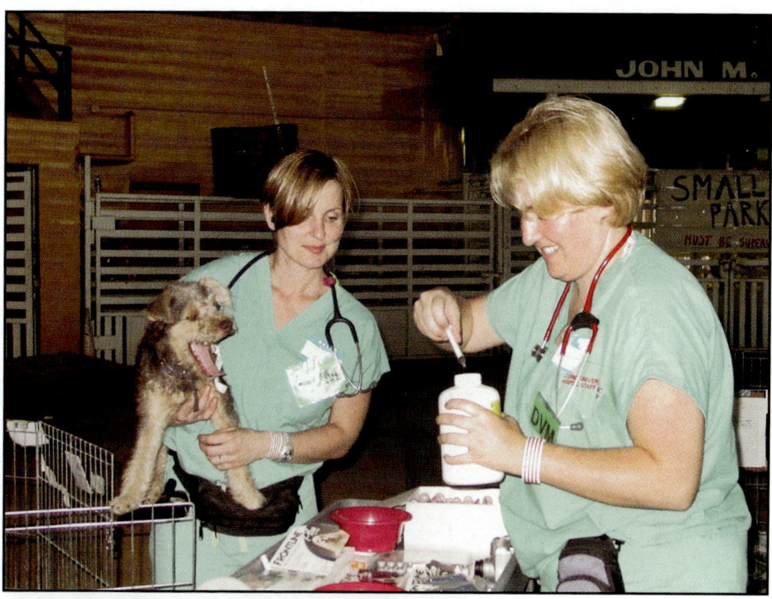

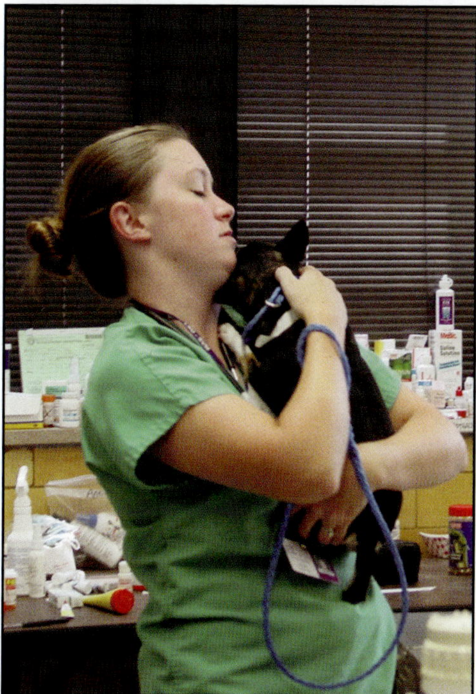

Veterinary colleges throughout the U.S. contacted the LSU vet school to offer their help in caring for animals rescued after Hurricane Katrina. **Above:** Volunteers from Cornell University's vet school attend to a canine evacuee. **Left:** LSU veterinary student Piper Lambard comforts a patient in the triage area.

– Photos courtesy of the LSU
School of Veterinary Medicine

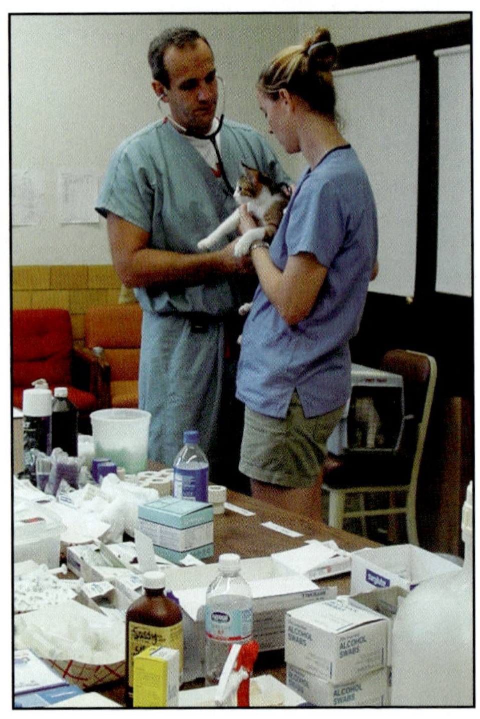

Veterinarian anesthesiologist Dr. Claudio Natalini and vet student Trinka Adamson examine a cat in the triage area of the temporary animal shelter set up on the LSU campus.

– Photos courtesy of the LSU
School of Veterinary Medicine

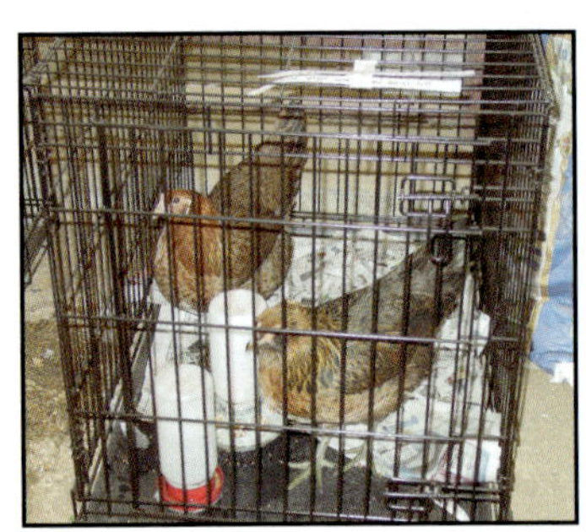

Not only were dogs and cats rescued after Hurricane Katrina but a number of chickens and ducks were scooped up as well.

The Rev. Jim Morrison and his dog, Blue, relax in St. Thomas Aquinas Church on Nicholls State University's campus in Thibodaux. When 130 Hurricane Katrina evacuees and their animals were denied access to a shelter in Thibodaux, Fr. Morrison invited them all to stay at the university's Catholic Center.

– Photo by Matt Stamey, *The Houma Courier*

Among the New Orleans area evacuees who took shelter at the St. Thomas Aquinas Catholic Center in Thibodaux were Karen Nelson and her pets, Toto and Katie.

– Photo courtesy of *The Nicholls Worth*

Judy Panessiti and her daughter, Jessica Juderman, were involved in numerous animal rescues in New Orleans after Hurricane Katrina. **Left:** *Jessica carries a pit bull to a rescue vehicle; the dog was too weak to walk.* **Below:** *A cocker spaniel, trapped for days in an above-ground swimming pool, was paddling for her life when Jessica found her. The exhausted dog was saved.*

– Photos by Judy Panessiti

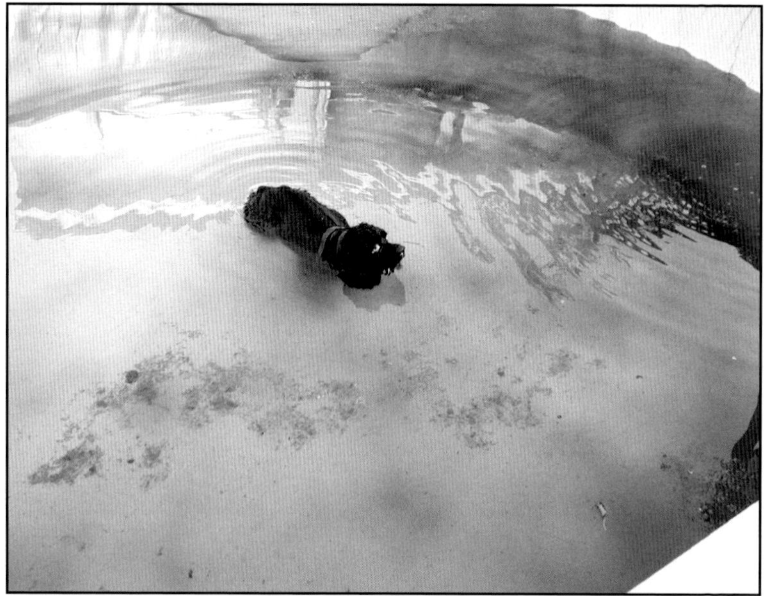

While human evacuees filled the Cajundome in Lafayette for Hurricane Katrina, their pets were cared for in nearby Blackham Coliseum. **Clockwise starting with photo below:** Hundreds of dogs and cats were kept in crates on the floor of the coliseum. New Orleanian Donnie Melton holds one of his cats. Lafayette animal control officer Michelle Rozas cuddles with her new friend. A shelter volunteer dries a puppy after its bath.

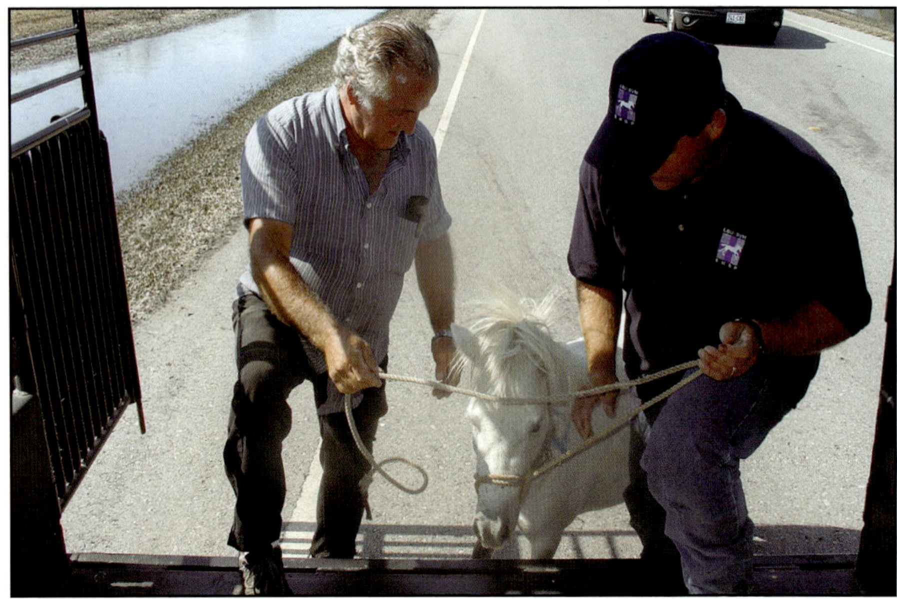

Horses and cattle were included in the animal rescue operation in south-west Louisiana following Hurricane Rita. Many weathered the storm while many more – especially cattle trapped between the Intracoastal Waterway and the Gulf's shoreline – perished in the storm surge.

– Photos courtesy of the LSU School of Veterinary Medicine

Dixon Center, many of the small animals were subsequently transported to shelters in cities around the country.

In addition to dogs and cats, significant numbers of horses and cattle were in need of rescue following the hurricanes. Hundreds of horses in the New Orleans area were brought to the Lamar Dixon Center, where they were examined, treated if need be, sheltered, fed and watered by volunteers. Numerous calls came in from people in Louisiana and neighboring states, offering help in the form of pastures, stalls, feed, hay and money.

Thousands of cattle, perhaps as many as 12,000, were drowned in Hurricane Rita's 15-foot tidal surge that inundated marshes and low-lying pastures in the coastal parishes of southwest Louisiana. Other cattle ran free on whatever high ground they could find.

Thousands of small animals were sheltered in other states as kind-hearted people from around the U.S. offered to care for the dogs and cats until they could be reunited with their owners. Pets were sent to shelters in St. Louis, San Diego, San Antonio and numerous other cities.

The rescue of these thousands of helpless animals proved to be a nationwide effort, teamwork for a cause that continues to touch the hearts of many, many people around the world.

Diary of an animal rescuer

My daughter and I joined the legions of people rescuing stranded and starving animals in the New Orleans area following Hurricane Katrina. It was a bittersweet experience that we'll remember for the rest of our lives.

By Judy Panessiti

Tuesday, September 20, 2005

The past couple of days have been very rewarding and very disturbing at the same time. Jess (Jessica Juderman, my daughter) and I feel that we have a message to get out there once we get back. There is so much frustration at the end of the day as the sun starts to give way to the moon.

Last night as we were leaving (yes, a wee bit past curfew) we had little doggies come up to the moving van and jump on it and bark non-stop, not once but several times. They are desperate for food, water and some human contact.

There was a dog barking in the distance from inside a home. We could hear the muffle but couldn't locate the home. That's first on our list today.

We found our first pup that tried to survive but didn't. She had been locked up in a little outdoor shed attached to a third-story apartment, on the balcony. Her owner locked her in thinking he would be back in a couple of days. She chewed her way through the wall (a very common story here) onto the balcony, only to starve to death.

I must say how very proud I am of my daughter. Her conviction and passion and her knowledge have been reassuring and encouraging. Just yesterday we had our golden moment – so far. We found this neighborhood that no one had been to yet. No one had checked homes for bodies. *Yikes!* I called out jestfully, in a delirious moment, "Hey all doggies, kitties and fishes, we are here to save you." And dogs ran out from everywhere! It was like carrying several loaves of bread near a pond of ducks and geese. They were everywhere. Jess went in one direction with Vienna sausage in hand and I in the other direction. She was after two Lhasa Apsos and I was after three big mixed breeds that were as skinny as alley cats.

All the animals run up to you, but they are afraid, very afraid. They won't let you within three feet of them without coaxing or cornering, and then they calm down.

Anyway, I am on my mission and I hear this bloodcurdling scream from Jess. "Mooooooooooom!" Parents, you know the one! I dropped everything, some worst fears running through my mind, and ran in her direction. As I came around my corner of the street, she came around the corner of the house where she was after the two dogs.

"A dog is in the pool!" She screamed out a list of things to grab from the van (Noah's Ark II, thanks to Boo, my sister) and ran back to the back yard of the house. I saw one dog in the crate in the van, so I thought the dog she was chasing ran from her and fell into the pool. I grabbed supplies and took off. She was on the deck of an above-ground pool. There was a dog in the pool, but it was not the dog she was chasing. That dog she was chasing brought her right up to this spot and started barking and barking and barking at the pool. He told her where to find a black cocker spaniel that was pitiful. It had been in this pool for many days, swimming and swimming. Its eyes were completly covered in this white, thick pus-like covering. It couldn't see a bit. My heart sank.

"Don't get upset now. We have to save her," Jess said firmly.

It took a bit of time, and Jess was half in the pool, but we got the pup out. She collapsed the second she hit the ground. She just didn't have anymore in her. I handed her a couple of Vienna sausages and she nearly took off my fingers out of starvation.

We got her back to the van, and again Jess went into action, cleaning the eyes, drying the coat, checking for any wounds. Then we went back for the dog that brought us to her. He ran and ran and ran. We ran and ran and ran. We were not leaving our little hero. We didn't understand why he brought us to the dog in the pool and then ran, but we weren't about to leave him. He didn't know just yet how tenacious Jess and I are. He never had a chance. He ran us around his neighborhood and back into the very yard where the other dog was. Jess climbed under a fallen fence where he had run for cover, and she snagged him. We picked him up and put him in the cage with the first Lhasa Apso and right next to the cage with the cocker spaniel.

If we don't save another life, this trip was worth saving that one pup that had been swimming for no telling how long and the pups that were standing guard looking for help in the only way they knew. (Yes, I am crying again!)

For those of you who know Jess personally, you will easily be able to imagine this next bit. We saved *everything*! Not one bird, fish, turtle or lizard was left behind. We have been blessed.

We didn't end up staying in the parking lot (the base of rescue operations). Family had lights and water about half a mile away. So, Jess turned their storage shed into a sanctuary of exotic animals: seven birds, two iguanas, about 35 fish from all over town and four turtles that are getting to know each other in one little cage.

The only thing we haven't saved at this point is a cat or snake. We have tried to catch some kitties, but the ones outside are just too afraid. We leave food and water.

We have pictures and we have stories, but we are off today to do what we can. They say we will only be able to save about one or two percent of the animals left behind.

Noah's Ark II signing off for now...

Lafayette people open their hearts to displaced pets

Blackham Coliseum shelters hundreds of animal evacuees driven out of New Orleans by Hurricane Katrina.

By Patricia Gannon

Donnie Melton is from River Ridge, an area between Kenner and New Orleans. A soft-spoken, self-sufficient Louisiana man, he not only rode out Hurricane Katrina but made his way safely to Lafayette in his van with his wife, three children, the family dog and four cats. While he seems like the kind of guy who usually can fend for himself, he needed a hand back in September after the storm.

"I suppose I could give up the cats if I have to," Melton said. "But I can't leave my dog."

Melton's five pets were among the hundreds of 4-legged evacuees being tended by volunteers at Blackham Coliseum's makeshift animal shelter in Lafayette. Animal control officer Michelle Rozas expected she and others would be caring for many of these animals for a long time to come.

"In 90 minutes, we registered 75 volunteers," she reported. "We filled a legal pad in three days and finally just had to turn them away. The community's response was awesome."

While two truckloads of dry food were unloaded in front of the coliseum, separate piles of cleaning supplies, canned food and pet toys were overflowing the outer areas of the facility. All was orderly, clean and surprisingly quiet, given the nature of the task and the magnitude of the disaster. Here and there a mournful howl signaled despair, but most animals kept a silent vigil, waiting for the sound of that special voice. Animal crates looked more like cradles – full of stuffed toys, knitted blankets and pillows. Sympathetic citizens arrived in a steady stream, bringing more food and more toys.

"We have groomers giving their time, donated food for the human volunteers, and people who come just to launder our clothes," said Rozas, who was on duty for long hours. "We even have a local woman rescuing the animals of emergency medical personnel who can't care for them temporarily."

Animals seeking refuge were given instant rabies vaccinations, wormings and shots to prevent bordetellosis, a highly contagious ailment commonly known as "kennel cough." Local veterinarians Toby Wexler, David Orgeron and Renee Poirier oversaw the relief effort, with the additional help of an evacuated veterinarian from Mandeville.

"Dr. Poirier and her vet techs are a godsend – organizing, keeping everyone on their toes, instructing volunteers, and even providing minimal services gratis to animals that have arrived with problems," Rozas stated.

Dr. Poirier, who is state animal response team coordinator for the Louisiana Veterinary Medical Association, had the daunting task of synchronizing shelter efforts in Alexandria, Shreveport, Monroe and Lafayette. She said the shelters weren't just for the animals' peace of mind.

"The Red Cross refuses pets at their facilities," Dr. Poirier explained. "People who are away from home, many never to return, also end up separated from an important source of comfort. Since owners are responsible for their pets' care at our shelters, they can stay with them during the day."

For a while, many animals traumatized by the evacuation were not eating or drinking, and even normally docile pets became aggressive in response to being separated from their owners.

"So far, there've been no major casualties," Rozas reported a few days after the shelter opened. "They sleep at night and are getting better acclimated."

Those running the shelter at Blackham Coliseum were expecting some of the dogs and cats to be abandoned before it was all over.

"We suspected it would be a problem, so we were prepared," Rozas said. "We started a list of people willing to adopt. There were releases to sign if you were no longer able to care for your pets, and we had an excellent adoption program."

It turned out that most owners came to get their pets by the time the shelter closed. Other owners came and said tearfully that they could no longer care for their pets and asked that a good home be found for them. Other owners simply never returned, for various reasons.

A special place of refuge for evacuees and their pets

When 130 evacuees and their animals were denied access to a shelter in Thibodaux, Fr. Jim Morrison cordially invited them all to stay in his church.

By Melanie Melancon

Many residents of the New Orleans area found shelter from Hurricane Katrina in the Stopher Gymnasium on the campus of Nicholls State University in Thibodaux. Those with pets, however, were denied access to the shelter.

So, 130 evacuees and their 150 pets remained outside of the shelter. The people were tired and dejected, many of them feeling a bit wounded over the treatment they received.

The outsiders and their pets were spotted by Fr. Jim Morrison, pastor of St. Thomas Aquinas Catholic Church, on Nicholls State's campus. Moved to compassion by their plight, he offered them all a place to stay – in his church!

"The only natural thing to say was, 'Just come to St. Thomas,'" Fr. Morrison says, referring to the St. Thomas Aquinas Catholic Center.

And so the people and their pets followed Fr. Morrison to the church. They made themselves comfortable as best they could, in the church itself and in the adjacent student center.

"It was almost like being in Noah's Ark," the 44-year-old priest recalls.

Despite the large number of people and pets and the lack of electricity, the first night in the church was quiet. There was "a hush of despair and exhaustion," Fr. Morrison reports. The candle-lit church was peaceful, as rottweilers mingled with

Chihuahuas, cats, birds, rabbits and even a pot-bellied pig, without fights or attacks.

Fr. Morrison was moved by the sight. He would later reflect on the experience:

"Our altar has never been adorned more beautifully than it is with these people and their animals seeking the sanctuary of God."

When the people of Thibodaux learned of the shelter, support poured in from local pet stores, veterinarians and animal lovers, who donated portable kennels, supplies, food and medical services. And when the news spread on a national level, people across America began sending contributions and letters of encouragement, some "signed" by their pets.

"It brought a lot of joy to our church," Fr. Morrison says.

Volunteers, including children, offered a helping hand by bathing and walking the animals and helping the evacuees find family members, serving food and offering medical care.

The experience removed barriers between people of different races, religions and income levels.

"All of a sudden, they became one," Fr. Morrison notes.

The evacuees were no longer residents of upscale New Orleans subdivisions or public housing projects, but pet owners who shared a similar love and concern for their animals.

It turned out that the Catholic student center was used as a shelter not only for a few nights but for more than a month. Many of the evacuees had no place to go because their homes were destroyed by the flooding of New Orleans.

In the weeks following the hurricane the shelter would be used by some 250 pet owners. With that many people and pets, some wear and tear was bound to occur, and it did. The church lawn looked like a barnyard, trampled and somewhat torn up. The carpet in the student center sustained tears and stains, some of the furniture was scratched and nicked, and fleas burrowed into the carpet. Additionally, the sound of barking could be heard on a regular basis during Fr. Morrison's sermons.

But none of this seemed to bother Fr. Morrison, the proud owner of a dog named Blue. In fact, if he had it to do all over again, he'd invite the people and their pets again, he says.

"That's what the church is built for – to care for people," he concludes.

<u>Epilogue</u>

Never say die

Ten years after the terrible storms of 2005 visited their wrath on south Louisiana, the two communities that sustained the greatest damage were still rebuilding, to one degree or another.

What Hurricane Katrina did to the greater New Orleans area and what Hurricane Rita did to the town of Cameron was staggering.

Katrina caused more than 1,800 deaths in the New Orleans area and on the Mississippi Gulf Coast and $135 billion in property damage. New Orleans' inadequate levee system was broken in many places, thousands upon thousands of homes were flooded severely, and the iconic Superdome was mauled outside and trashed inside.

Some in the national media speculated that the dome would have to be demolished. New Orleans Saints owner Tom Benson was seriously considering moving the team to San Antonio, then to Los Angeles, permanently. A college professor from St. Louis University told CBS News it made no sense to try to rebuild New Orleans because, being well below sea level, it would be subject to yet another cataclysmic flood.

A month after Katrina struck, Hurricane Rita slammed the southwest corner of Louisiana and mowed down virtually every building in Cameron, the parish seat of Cameron Parish.

For Cameron and New Orleans, the job of recovering and rebuilding seemed hopeless. It looked for all the world that Cameron had been dealt a death blow and that New Orleans was so critically injured that it could never recover.

But hope springs eternal.

Shortly after Katrina, New Orleans began rebuilding – after its citizens got over the initial shock of seeing their city in ruins. Billions of dollars of Federal aid began pouring in, and volunteers from around the nation flocked to the crippled city to assist with its rehabilitation.

First aid was administered by the Federal government in the form of blue tarps for damaged roofs (thousands of them) and little white travel trailers (tens of thousands of units), as well as food stamps, cash cards and unemployment funds. The U.S. Army Corps of Engineers began what turned out to be a $14.5 billion upgrade of the levee system. A new University Medical Center and a new Veterans Administration hospital were built, each costing $1 billion. Roads and bridges were refurbished, and some 100,000 houses were restored.

The much-publicized and -criticized Road Home Program provided nearly $9 billion to rebuild – or to purchase – damaged houses. Despite an abundance of bureaucratic entanglements and frustrations, in the long run the program helped many, many to return home, as intended.

One project that got extraordinary attention was the repair and enhancement of the Superdome. Governor Kathleen Blanco, among others, felt that the Superdome was a symbol of hope for the future of New Orleans. If the job could be done very well and in relatively short order, the success of this project would surely lift the downtrodden spirits of the citizens of New Orleans. So, the construction work was given the highest of priorities and funded quickly to the tune of $300 million-plus of Federal and State money. The dome opened just in time for the Saints to host the Atlanta Falcons on Sept. 25, 2006. The team was up for the game – way up – and so were the fans. The Falcons didn't stand a chance.

And New Orleans continued to recover. For the tenth anniversary of Katrina, the city's population stood at 384,000 – 90% of its pre-Katrina number. Sales tax income was higher than in 2005. Tourism industry revenue set a record of nearly $7 billion in 2014.

Meanwhile, in Cameron Parish, the population 10 years after Hurricane Rita was only 6,800 – just two-thirds of the 10,000 it had before the storm. Interestingly, on any given day in 2015, there were some 8,000 construction workers in the parish – more than there were permanent residents. Most of the workers were building facilities for the processing and exporting of liquefied natural gas, according to Clair Hebert Marceaux, director of economic development for the parish.

In 2015, the parish had three grocery stores, five gas stations, four restaurants, four libraries, three national wildlife refuges and "six alligators for each person living here," Ms. Marceaux reported.

After the storm, many residents of the town of Cameron opted against rebuilding in their former hometown and instead moved north, to villages further from the coast. The Federal government provided more than $150 million for the construction or repair of public facilities, including fire stations and recreation centers.

So, life goes on in Cameron Parish and in the greater New Orleans area. While neither has been fully restored to its pre-storm status, progress continues to be made. It's clear that American ingenuity lives here.

– Trent Angers

Appendix 1

No pet left behind
(*It's the law now*)

Images of the horrific aftermath of Hurricane Katrina provided the impetus for the law requiring the evacuation, transportation and care of companion animals in times of disaster.

The national media's wall to wall coverage of Hurricane Katrina and its aftermath in 2005 produced many shocking and heart-rending pictures of desperate people and helpless pets.

Among the most pitiful scenes was a sobbing 9-year-old boy being forced to leave behind his little white dog "Snowball" as the boy was being ushered onto an evacuation bus at the Louisiana Superdome.

At the time, there were no laws in place that addressed the need to evacuate and care for companion animals following natural disasters.

But that has changed.

Among the millions watching TV when the boy was separated from his dog at the Superdome was California Congressman Tom Lantos, a passionate advocate for the well-being of animals. He was so moved by the scene that he immediately went to work drafting a bill that would provide for the evacuation of animals in natural disasters. He was joined in authoring the bill by Congressman Chris Shays of Connecticut. Sponsors of the Senate bill were Sen. Ted Stevens of Alaska and Sen. Frank Lautenberg of New Jersey.

The bill was signed into law by President George Bush in the fall of 2006, and by 2011 it had been adopted by more than 30 states, including Louisiana.

The bill is known as the **Pet Evacuation and Transportation Safety Act**, the PETS Act. Its main provisions include:

- Local and State emergency preparedness authorities must include plans for pets and service animals in their disaster plans - if local and State governmental entities are going to be eligible for disaster relief grants from the Federal Emergency Management Agency (FEMA).

- FEMA is given the authority to assist State and local governments in developing disaster relief plans to accommodate people who have pets and service animals.

- Federal funds are authorized to help create emergency shelters for pets.

- FEMA is authorized to assist people with pets and service animals, as well as the animals, following major natural disasters.

Happy about the quick passage of the national legislation, animal advocacy group leaders expressed optimism for the humane treatment of animals – and their owners – following future disasters.

"While Katrina wreaked so much devastation and disruption, it also highlighted the remarkable bond between this nation and our pets and service animals – and the need for public policy to echo that appreciation of animals," Wayne Pacelle, president and CEO of The Humane Society of the United States, said shortly after the passage of the PETS Act.

Pacelle noted that previous governmental failure to include pets in pre-disaster planning cost not only animals their lives but also people.

"People lost their lives in the wake of Katrina because government responders told them their animals had to be left behind – and they couldn't bear to abandon their pets," Pacelle said. "For many people who face losing everything, their pet is the only comfort they have left."

THE BLESSING CUP: Every family strives to strengthen its bonds by mutually sharing hopes and fears, joys and sorrows. The blessing cup is a family tradition you can begin in your home to help you toward this goal. It is a sign of solidarity, of oneness in prayer and purpose. The blessing cup service is centered around a common cup and based on the use of Scripture and petition. The cup is made of metal, pottery or glass and should be filled with a beverage that fits the occasion and the taste of the participants. All in attendance should drink from the cup. It is kept in a prominent place in the home as a reminder of the family's mutual hope. It is used as the family gathers for prayer at special times – holidays, birthdays, anniversaries; times of change, growth and loss. – Rock Travnikar, OFM

<u>Appendix 2</u>

Funeral Service For A Pet
(In the Christian Tradition)

From the book, *The Blessing Cup*,
by Rock Travnikar, OFM (Franciscan priest)

Opening Prayer

> Master and Lord of all creation, hear the prayer we offer you in the name of the Father, and of the Son, and of the Holy Spirit.

Scripture

> Are not five sparrows sold for two pennies? Yet not one of them is forgotten in God's sight. (Luke 12:6)

Petitions

> You have shown us affection and faithfulness through all of creation. We are grateful as we pray.

> *Response:* Comfort us, Lord.

> We remember the laughter and joy which ___________ has given us, and we pray.

> Help us to share kindness and care with all living things, we pray.

> *Add your own petitions.*

Collect

> In your goodness you have called us to be stewards of all creation. We take up this cup, grateful for having been entrusted with the care of this creature. We marvel at how you have fashioned and formed our world in harmony and peace.

Sharing of the Blessing Cup

Pray together the Our Father.

Index

Note: Page numbers in *italics* refer to maps, photographs
or content within the captions of photographs.

From Bags to Riches
How the New Orleans Saints and the people of their hometown rose from the depths together

The inspiring story of the New Orleans Saints' 2009-2010 football season that culminated with the winning of the Super Bowl. The book explains how the struggling NFL team and the storm-weary people of New Orleans and the Gulf Coast lifted one another's spirits – and fortunes – in the post-Hurricane Katrina years, 2006 – 2010. The narrative is a study in contrasting moods, ranging from the depression and despair that come with being victims of the worst natural disaster in U.S. history, to the euphoria that accompanies the winning of the Super Bowl after 43 years of mostly losing seasons. (Author: Jeff Duncan ISBN: 0-925417-68-8. Price: $24.95)

Blessed Be Jazz
The Story of My Life as a Clarinet-Playing Jesuit Priest in The French Quarter of New Orleans

The 192-page hardcover autobiography of Rev. Frank Coco, SJ (1920-2006), a Jesuit priest who served for more than 50 years in south Louisiana as a retreat director, high school teacher and jazz musician. Using his clarinet, he performed extensively in New Orleans nightclubs, sitting in with some of the best-known jazz musicians of his time, including Ronnie Kole, Al Hirt and Pete Fountain. (Author: Rev. Frank Coco, SJ. ISBN: 0-925417-89-0. Price: $19.95)

Tiger Beat
Covering LSU sports for 35 years

A 240-page hardcover book by a veteran sportswriter who covered LSU football and basketball for Baton Rouge, La., newspapers for 35 years. It features the head coaches over a 50-year span, starting in the mid-1950s, as well as big games and top athletes, including the "Chinese Bandits," Billy Cannon, "Pistol Pete" Maravich, Chris Jackson and Shaquille O'Neal. (Author: Sam King. ISBN: 0-925417-85-8. Price $22.95)

Getting Over the 4 Hurdles of Life

A 160-page hardcover book that shows us ways to get past the obstacles, or hurdles, that block our path to success, happiness and peace of mind. Four of the most common hurdles are: "I can't / You can't," past failures or fear of failure, handicaps, and lack of self-knowledge. This inspiring book – by one of the top motivational speakers in the U.S. – is brought to life by intriguing stories of various people who overcame life's hurdles. (Author: Coach Dale Brown. ISBN: 0-925417-72-6. Price: $17.95)

Southern Jesuit Biographies

A 256-page hardcover book containing brief biographies of 220 Jesuit priests and brothers who served the people of the Southeastern and Southwestern U.S. Spanning a period of some 300 years, their work included teaching in schools and colleges, preaching the Gospel, building churches and schools, administering the sacraments, leading retreats, working with the poor, and promoting peace and justice. The book is well-illustrated with photographs, both historic and contemporary, as well as maps. (Authors: Rev. Jerome Neyrey, S.J., and Rev. Thomas Clancy, S.J. ISBN: 0-925417-92-0. Price: $40.00)

Grand Coteau
The Holy Land of South Louisiana

A 176-page hardcover book that captures the spirit of one of the truly holy places in North America. It is a town of mystery, with well-established ties to the supernatural, including the famous Miracle of Grand Coteau. Brought to life by dozens of exceptional color photographs, the book focuses on the town's major religious institutions: The Academy of the Sacred Heart, Our Lady of the Oaks Retreat House and St. Charles College/Jesuit Novitiate. The book explores not only the history of these three institutions but also the substance of their teachings. (Author: Trent Angers. ISBN: 0-925417-47-5. Price: $44.95)

The Forgotten Hero of My Lai
The Hugh Thompson Story (Revised Edition)

The 272-page hardcover book that tells the story of the U.S. Army helicopter pilot who risked his life to rescue South Vietnamese civilians and to put a stop to the My Lai massacre during the Vietnam War in 1968. Revised Edition shows President Nixon initiated the effort to sabotage the My Lai massacre trials so no U.S. soldier would be convicted of a war crime. (Author: Trent Angers. ISBN: 0-925417-90-4. Price: $22.95)

The Elephant Man
A Study in Human Dignity

A 138-page softcover book whose first edition inspired the movie and the Tony Award-winning play by the same name. This fascinating story, which has touched the hearts of readers throughout the world for over a century, is now complete with the publication of this, the Third Edition. Illustrated with photos and drawings of The Elephant Man. (Author: Ashley Montagu. ISBN: 0-925417-41-6. Price: $12.95.)

TO ORDER, list the books you wish to purchase along with the corresponding cost of each. Add $4 per book for shipping & handling. Louisiana residents add 8% tax to the cost of the books. Mail your order and check or credit card authorization (VISA/MC/AmEx) to: Acadian House Publishing, Dept. TS05, P.O. Box 52247, Lafayette, LA 70505. Or call (800) 850-8851. To order online, go to www.acadianhouse.com.